High-Stakes Testing and the Decline of Teaching and Learning

Critical Education Policy and Politics
Series Editor: Michael A. Peters

This series focuses on current issues in education. Books will explore the development of the new educational policies and practices that are changing the structure and functions of educational institutions—primary, secondary, and higher—both here and abroad. In the United States, the new federal involvement in primary and secondary education, most conspicuously in the passage of the No Child Left Behind legislation, has brought a new era of testing and accountability while raising questions about the role of schools in promoting social inclusion and providing basic training for the new "information" economy. Books will explore such hot topics as charter schools, testing, vouchers and tax deductions for education, teacher education and the teaching profession, and public–private competition, to name a few. The series is committed to publishing high-quality, innovative, and original work that adopts a critical view of education policy and seeks to view it within the wider parameters of contemporary public policy discussions.

Titles in the Series:

Building Knowledge Cultures: Education and Development in the Age of Knowledge Capitalism, Michael A. Peters with A. C. (Tina) Besley

High-Stakes Testing and the Decline of Teaching and Learning: The Real Crisis in Education, David Hursh

High-Stakes Testing and the Decline of Teaching and Learning

The Real Crisis in Education

DAVID HURSH

ROWMAN & LITTLEFIELD PUBLISHERS, INC.
Lanham • Boulder • New York • Toronto • Plymouth, UK

ROWMAN & LITTLEFIELD PUBLISHERS, INC.

Published in the United States of America
by Rowman & Littlefield Publishers, Inc.
A wholly owned subsidary of The Rowman & Littlefield Publishing Group, Inc.
4501 Forbes Boulevard, Suite 200, Lanham, Maryland 20706
www.rowmanlittlefield.com

Estover Road
Plymouth PL6 7PY
United Kingdom

British Library Cataloguing in Publication Information Available

Library of Congress Cataloging-in-Publication Data:

Hursh, David W., 1948–
  High-stakes testing and the decline of teaching and learning : the real crisis in
education / David Hursh.
    p. cm.
  Includes bibliographical references.
  ISBN-13: 978-0-7425-6148-9 (cloth : alk. paper)
  ISBN-10: 0-7425-6148-8 (cloth : alk. paper)
  ISBN-13: 978-0-7425-6149-6 (pbk. : alk. paper)
  ISBN-10: 0-7425-6149-6 (pbk. : alk. paper)
  1. Educational tests and measurements—United States. I. Title.
  LB3051.H89 2008
  371.260973—dc22   2007045223

Printed in the United States of America

⊗™ The paper used in this publication meets the minimum requirements of American
National Standard for Information Sciences—Permanence of Paper for Printed Library
Materials, ANSI/NISO Z39.48-1992.

Contents

Acknowledgments

While books may have a single author, they often reflect the author's relationship with friends and colleagues. This is especially true of books as autobiographical as this one. Many of the people whose insights and wisdom I have benefited from are identified in the text. Others not identified in the text are no less important.

As I describe, my interest in education began as an undergraduate student in Kansas, particularly while working at the alternative university. Thanks go to Sue Maes and Sally Wisely for their support as colleagues. I began teaching elementary school in Nebraska and then returned to Kansas to start my own school. In those two settings I learned from some great teachers: Sue Sandmeyer, Neil Shanker, Esther Gray, Camille Gontarek, Ken Haar, and Carol Baumert. During those same years, I became friends with Jonathan Kozol and Herb Kohl, who supported my efforts in educational reform and writing.

While teaching elementary school, Elizabeth Vallance introduced me to the publications of Michael Apple, Ken Zeichner, and Herbert Kliebard, all at the University of Wisconsin–Madison, which led me to pursue a doctorate in education. Michael, Ken, Herb, and Erik Olin Wright (sociology) all served on my doctoral committee, and I still frequently turn to Michael and Ken for advice (a professor's mentorship never ends). Moreover, the quality of one's doctoral experience depends on the quality of his fellow doctoral students, and no one could have had more supportive colleagues than I had. Thanks go to Susan Noffke, Marie Brennan, James Ladwig, Henry St. Maurice, Dan Liston, Cameron McCarthy, and Jennifer Gore for their high standards that have always inspired me.

My research and writing has been supported by numerous colleagues from around the world: Marilyn Cochran-Smith, Gloria Ladson-Billings, Michael Peters, Fazal Rizvi, Christine Sleeter, Bob Lingard, Linda McNeil, Angela Valenzuela, E. Wayne Ross, Sandra Mathison, Stephen Fleury, Kevin Vinson, Tom Pedronio, Joao Paraskeva, Mark Pryn, Sandra Hollingsworth, and John Smyth. Thanks also to Pauline Lipman. Pauline epitomizes what it means to be a scholar and activist and how to combine social theory and critique.

In fall 2004, thanks to the current dean, Raffaella Borasi, I finally received the junior leave that I was promised sixteen years earlier, and Camille Martina (my wife and fellow scholar) and I embarked for Bristol, England, to spend five months studying with two of the world's top scholars, Roger Dale and Susan Robertson, on globalization and education. During our England trip, we worked with many great colleagues, but I would like to single out Sally Tomlinson, Dave Hill, David Gillborn, Deborah Youdell, Sandra Leaton Gray, and Martin Thrupp.

I also want to acknowledge the support of two former Warner School colleagues, Ann Monroe-Baillargeon and Bruce Kimball, and two new colleagues, Andrew Wall and Abe DeLeon. Theresa Danylak, a Warner School staff member in communications, provided editorial assistance throughout the final writing of the text.

Over the last eight years, I have focused on not only talking about education policy, but also working to change policy, and I had the good fortune to work with Monty Neill from Fairtest, Deborah Meier, and Michelle Fine. Furthermore, eight years ago a group of Rochester educators and I began the Coalition for Common Sense in Education. The group included Bill Cala, who as the former superintendent of the Fairport (NY) schools and now the interim superintendent of the Rochester City Schools (NY) is one of the most courageous individuals I know; Dan Drmacich, principal of Rochester's School Without Walls; Rich Ryan, whose research on motivation refutes high-stakes testing; and Doug Noble, a teacher and scholar.

Many Warner School students have read drafts of these chapters, in particular the students in Camille's education foundations course, including

Zachary Keller, Gabe Chodak, Stephen Thorndike, Chris Wuest, Claudia Scott, and Kathryn Shaw. Thanks also to my doctoral assistant, Jason Blokius, who has read more drafts of this and other articles than I am sure he cares to remember. Furthermore, many of my former and current doctoral students have supported my efforts: Rebecca Goldstein, Catherine Compton-Lilly, Anne Perrault, Aggie Seneway, Deborah Hoeft, Michael Baker, Karen Soanes, and Jeanne Loysen.

My twin brother, Donald (aka DD), significantly influenced my early career decisions by introducing me to existential philosophy and political protest. My mom, Helen, helped demystify second grade.

Of course, none of this would have been possible without the unlimited support of the love of my life, Camille Martina, who is sharing this adventure with me.

1

Situating the Personal in the Political

I never wanted to be a teacher. In high school I constantly counted the minutes until the last bell, when I would be free to join the other boys playing whichever sport the season demanded. I measured my success not by test grades but by touchdowns and runs scored.

Therefore, I am surprised that for the last almost forty years I have been teaching. But it is in teaching, in the crucible of the classroom, that one can engage in asking questions and making sense of one another and the world. It is in the classroom where five- and six-year-olds respond to my question of how the Grand Canyon was formed with the unexpected but understandable explanation of earthquakes and tornadoes. And it is in last night's classroom of doctoral students—mostly teachers and administrators—where we deliberate the effect that the current testing movement has on our ability to engage students in making sense of the world around them.

However, beginning most recently with the release of *A Nation at Risk* in 1983, many corporate and governmental leaders have argued that our schools are in decline and can only be remedied by establishing standards, standardized testing, and accountability. In this book I assert that while our schools need to be improved, the recent reforms, including No Child Left Behind (NCLB), create the real crisis in education. By constructing a "manufactured crisis in education" (Berliner & Biddle, 1995), high-stakes testing, accountability, rewards, and punishments undermine recent gains in teaching and

learning and, by focusing on learning narrowly defined by test scores, negatively transform education to an extent that was unimaginable before the current reform movement.

Furthermore, the recent education reforms are part of a larger effort by
some corporate and political leaders to transform the nature of society by repealing the social democratic policies that have guided the United States for
much of the last century (policies that, while inadequate, have improved the
overall education and economic levels for Americans) in the belief that they
interfere with individual liberty and the efficiency of the marketplace; or, as
George W. Bush succinctly summarized, "Trade and markets are freedom"
(Fischer, 1999, cited in Schwarz, 2005, p. 4). Instead, the reformers desire to
implement policies that support markets and privatize public services.

Consequently, some economists (Friedman, 1995), politicians, and jour-
nalists (Goldberg, 2007) demand that the public school—what they pejora-
tively label "government schools"— "monopoly" be eliminated and that the
entire educational system from preschool through university be privatized
(Johnson & Salle, 2004). Others, including the current Bush administration,
have proposed voucher programs and charter schools as an intermediate step
between public schooling and total privatization. Together, then, the rise of
high-stakes testing and accountability with the gradual and potentially total
privatization of public schools compose the real crisis in education.

In defending public schools, I do not want to romanticize the state of education previous to the recent wave of reforms. During my forty years as an educator I have criticized schools as asking little from students beyond
memorization and for failing to develop critical, knowledgeable citizens. Furthermore, as critics have documented (Kozol, 1967, 1991, 2005; Kohl, 1967;
Anyon, 1997), the educational system continues to fail many students from
working-class families and students of color in schools that are, to a large degree, separate and unequal. Our political system fails to provide adequate
funding to many urban schools and, consequently, students lack both adequately prepared teachers and resources such as textbooks and technology.
Moreover, schools have often ignored and been contemptuous of students
who embody culture that is not white and middle class. Consequently, families with students in urban schools have sometimes led calls for educational
markets and standardized testing (Pedroni, 2007).

However, based on my own experiences, as I will describe, with successful urban schools such as the Urban Academy[1] in New York City and the School Without Walls in Rochester, New York, my view is that public schools can and must serve all children. The classroom should be a place in which we raise questions about complicated issues (such as global warming, war, economics, and language), engage in debates, and come to tentative conclusions; a place where we can assess and appreciate not only what we know but also what others know, a place in which we learn how to live together democratically in the interests of the common good. Schools can and should contribute to creating a more equal, inclusive, and socially just world. There is much that can be improved, and in later chapters I provide some examples of reforms worth pursuing.

I support, therefore, what Kincheloe (2001) refers to as "standards of complexity" that examine knowledge holistically, within the context of our relationship to the world (p. 90). I support high standards, standards higher than those that can be assessed via a standardized exam. I am not against using standardized exams as one of multiple measures. But, I am against high-stakes standardized tests that are used to punish students, teachers, schools, and school districts and used to misrepresent public schools as failures beyond redemption. I am against the subsequent narrowing and simplification of the curriculum as schools focus on preparing students to pass the tests, rather than to obtain a complex and sophisticated understanding of the world.

As I will describe, students in New York, where I teach, have endured an increasing number of standardized tests. Previous to the passage of NCLB in early 2002, students initially confronted passing nine standardized exams in grades four through eight and passing five standardized exams for high school graduation—one each in English, math, science, U.S. history, and global studies. With the passage of NCLB, students now face twenty-one exams before they enter high school. Increasingly, classrooms are places in which teachers and students act out the script given to them by someone else, neither teachers nor students ask the questions that matter, and learning is equated with passing a test.

Moreover, the exams themselves pose only a small part of the problem. Previous to NCLB, some states tied exams to school and district assessments with rewards and sanctions depending on results. But, with the passage of NCLB, the federal government has imposed numerous restrictions on schools and districts in terms of curricula and assessment, teacher education requirements, student privacy, and extracurricular activities. In addition, schools and districts failing to make "adequately yearly progress" face having their administration privatized, tutoring outsourced to for- and nonprofit corporations and religious institutions, and conversion to a charter school.

While education seems perennially in crisis, leading many teachers to hope that the recent reforms, like past reforms, will, in time, simply go away, the current reforms differ from past reforms in three significant ways. First, high-stakes testing, accountability, and privatization are part of a larger effort by corporate and political leaders to transform government's role in society, particularly whether and how it provides for individual welfare. With the arrival of the Reagan administration in the 1980s, politicians, economists, and corporate leaders began to more visibly promote neoliberal theories and polices, which promote economic profit and growth over all other social goals and avow that such goals are achieved by deregulating the economy, liberalizing trade, and dismantling public services by privatizing them. Neoliberal policies also aim to revoke the education, housing, workplace safety, and voting rights won by workers, women, and people of color from the 1930s to the 1970s. Neoliberalism forms the basis for privatizing, if not eliminating social services, such as Social Security, penal institutions, and other programs, and for passing free trade agreements such as the North American Free Trade Agreement (NAFTA).

Similarly, neoliberalism provides the rationale for reforming school curriculum and pedagogy to focus on teaching students the skills and knowledge they need to be productive workers; for adopting education policies, such as NCLB, in which "failing" schools may be administered by private corporations or converted to charter schools; and for funding private schools through voucher programs (Schemo, 2006).

In addition, not only does neoliberalism transform societal and educational goals, and the purposes and responsibilities of government, but it also transforms the way in which societal decisions are made. Neoliberalism replaces community deliberations over what we desire from society and our institutions with decisions made through the market. For example, rather than discussing what we want from our public schools, our preferences are indicated through which "school of choice" we send our children.

Throughout most of the world, neoliberalism has become the dominant view (Harvey, 2005). In the United States, it has become the dominant political ideology, even though neoliberalism, which forms the basis for the ideology, is rarely explicitly acknowledged. Consequently, repealing NCLB and similar policies requires not only resisting them on educational grounds but also asserting that the purpose of education is to promote economic growth and that privatization and markets are the appropriate ways to provide for the common good.

Second, the recent reforms, such as NCLB, systematically transform curricula, pedagogy, and assessment as a whole. Accountability requires, as argued by the neoliberal reformers, giving standardized tests to students so that administrators can use classroom, school, and district aggregate scores to reward or punish teachers and schools, and parents can use the scores to assess school quality. Given the high-stakes nature of the tests, many schools and school districts focus not on learning, but on raising test scores and developing or adopting standardized, often scripted, curricula to prepare students for the exams. As a result, adopting curricula and pedagogical approaches responsive to the interests, experiences, and needs of the students and teachers becomes difficult, if not impossible, because such changes require either eliminating or reducing the significance of the standardized exams. Resisting any part of the recent reforms requires resisting all of the reforms.

Lastly, repealing the recent wave of reforms may be difficult because the emphasis on scripted curriculum and teaching to the test substantially de-skills and de-professionalizes teachers; we may soon have few teachers capable of developing and implementing their own lessons and units. Before long, teaching may no longer exist as a profession in which the practitioners have substantial input and control of what they do.

Therefore, the current education reforms imposed on schools by cities, states, and the federal government are the most significant in the history of the United States. They threaten to radically undermine not only teaching and learning but also the future of public schools. It is these reforms that constitute the real crisis in education to which I want to respond.

Furthermore, it is ironic and disheartening that these regressive reforms are being imposed just as the last several decades of efforts by progressive educational researchers and reformers were beginning to make a positive difference. We now better understand how students learn (see, for example, Newman,

Griffin & Cole, 1989; Cazden, 1988), have developed innovative public schools that have demonstrated success at educating all students (schools such as the Urban Academy and Central Park East in New York City come to mind), and until the recent focus on basic skills and standardized tests, had been closing the achievement gap between white middle-class students and working-class students of color (Orfield, 2006).

Therefore, in this book I want to reaffirm teaching as a profession that attracts the intellectually talented and the morally courageous. I want to reaffirm teaching and learning as a way of combating a society that poet Adrienne Rich (1993) describes as smelling "of timidity, docility, demoralization, acceptance of the unacceptable" (p. xv); a society in which Rich sees, "the general public disarray of thinking, of feeling—an atrophy of our power to imagine other ways of navigating into our collective future"; a society "where every public decision has to be justified in the scales of corporate profits" (p. xvii).

Moreover, while neoliberalism, with its focus on markets, privatization, and competition, has become a dominant approach to governance and education, we must not accept the argument that it is inevitable. As I will describe, resistance to neoliberal policies has taken many forms globally, resulting in the modification, rejection, and replacement of neoliberal polices. Educators and community groups in Chicago are critiquing and developing alternatives to Renaissance 2010, which aims to remake Chicago into a global, neoliberal city. Elsewhere, groups in New York have worked to reform state education policies and NCLB.

In the chapters that follow, I interweave the personal and the political. The first story is my own in which I describe my transition from a working-class boy more interested in athletics than academics, who counted the hours and years before he would be free of school, to an adult engaged in a lifelong pursuit to improve education and teaching. It is the story of beginning, as a university student in the 1960s, to imagine that teaching could be part of a larger effort to create a more humane world. While I was not so naïve as to believe that developing new approaches to teaching and schooling would by itself change the world, I did believe, like John Dewey, that schools, as institutions that incorporated democratic decision making, could be places in which we learned to be democratic citizens. I, along with many others creating alternatives within and outside the public schools and those active in the civil rights movement and efforts to end the Vietnam War, had a vision of a more caring, less hierarchical world.

But now, more than three decades later, I acknowledge not only that the barriers to creating a more humane world are greater than I thought but also that they are greater than before. The movement toward high-stakes testing and accountability has removed educational questions from the classroom and situated them within state and federal bureaucracies. Teachers are evaluated not on whether they engaged students in meaningful learning but on whether they raised their students' test scores. In New York, for example, fourth-grade teachers (the grade in which, previous to NCLB, the first state standardized literacy and math tests were required) devote weeks, if not months, to preparing students for the test. Teachers are explicitly told not to take students to art and music classes, to put off social studies and science until after the test, and if it is not on the test, not to teach it. Further, the purpose of schooling is increasingly described as producing students who can contribute to the economic marketplace, who benefit the economy. Education is more complicated and political than I imagined.

Therefore, the second story I tell is about the changing nature of not only schools but also society. I describe as case studies recent reforms at the city, state, and federal levels, focusing on Chicago (Lipman, 2004, 2005), New York, Texas, and NCLB. I situate the reforms within the changing nature of governmental policies, in particular the shift from social democratic liberalism, which prevailed from the Roosevelt administration into the 1970s, to the neoliberalism that has dominated since the Reagan administration. We decreasingly think about democracy and our commitment to one another in terms of community and the common good, and instead conceptualize democracy as the individual rationally choosing within a competitive marketplace. Such a conception undermines the last century's efforts toward equality. In critiquing the rise of neoliberalism in general and education in particular, I also examine the specific language or discourses that are used by those promoting the recent testing and accountability reforms in an effort to reveal how the public is being persuaded to adopt policies that may not be in their best interests.

While the corporate and political forces I describe increasingly restrict teachers' decision making, and in many ways make teaching a less-attractive career, my goal is not to lament what has been lost. Rather, my goal is to describe what is possible, to critique the increasing emphasis on markets, accountability, and high-stakes standardized testing, and to describe what we might do to reclaim education as a profession. I hope to provide some ways of analyzing our classroom practices, our educational theories, and our state and national politics so that we can reclaim the agenda and work toward democratic schools and a democratic society.

In chapter 2, I describe how I, like Dewey, came to realize that the kinds of questions I was beginning to ask as a university student—questions about the nature of knowledge, learning, and the democratic process—could be explored in schools. These questions came about in part because of the difficulties I faced as a working-class student navigating first through high school and later university education. As I reflected on my own experiences, I began, as sociologist C. Wright Mills (1959) describes, to connect my "personal troubles" with "social structures," to ask questions about the structure of society, where society stands in human history, and who holds power in society (p. 6). For me, teaching became a place where I asked not only pedagogical questions but also sociological, philosophical, and political ones.

I also share my experiences as a working-class student because as educators we need to remember that many students come to school unaware of how classrooms and schools "work," and, therefore, need to learn not only what is in the curriculum but also about the culture of schools and the middle class. I describe the key role that other students played in my gaining social capital—relationships that could help me understand how to navigate school and society—and cultural capital, the knowledge necessary to succeed in schools. I also describe that as a university student in the 1960s, while I often treaded on the limits of what the university found politically acceptable, some administrators engaged students and faculty in conversations about whose knowledge should be in the curriculum and, in response, developed some new courses and programs. The chapter ends with the questions that I posed for myself regarding curriculum, teaching, and learning on the evening before my first day teaching in an elementary classroom.

My evolving answers to my questions in chapter 2 form the basis for chapter 3, where I describe some of my experiences as an elementary teacher. I do not pretend that my teaching is either typical or exemplary. Rather, I want to suggest that the kinds of questions Dewey raised about education and teaching are the kinds of questions that teachers need to continually raise if we are to develop democratic schools and a democratic society.

In chapter 4, I argue that what education should represent and how it should be organized has never and will never be agreed upon. But beginning in the early twentieth century, education became increasingly contested, most significantly between those who built on the social efficiency movement that Frederick Winslow Taylor (1911) initiated—arguing that students should be prepared to be productive workers—and those who argued that the purpose of education was to prepare students for democratic citizenship (Kliebard, 2004). I cite the 1915 debate between David Snedden, a powerful state commissioner of education, and John Dewey, a leading advocate of education for democratic citizenship, for the clarity in which they describe the issues. The current emphasis on preparing students to be workers within a global society and implementing city, state, and national systems of standardized testing and accountability extend social efficiency into schools to a degree previously unimaginable.

As stated previously, neoliberal theories and policies are central to the rise of the current educational reforms. Therefore, in that chapter I also provide an overview of neoliberalism, how it complements but is not the same as globalization, how it came about, how it differs from previous conceptions of society, and the neoliberal basis for recent education reforms. I also briefly describe some of the contradictions and failures of neoliberals, which I expand upon in the concluding chapter when I discuss some of the ways in which neoliberalism is being resisted and rejected.

Given that, as I will show, neoliberalism benefits primarily the already privileged to the detriment of most everyone else, one of the questions worth asking is how have these reforms been successfully implemented? In chapter 5, I examine the recent educational reforms in New York and Texas and at the federal level with NCLB. In particular, I show that proponents of the recent reforms (*reform* itself is one of those "weasel words" [Hall, 1998] that is used to garner support—who argues against reform?—but may be meaningless) assert that standardized tests and accountability are required by increasing global economic competition, that the reforms will improve educational and economic equality, and that they provide for more objective forms of assessment than those provided by teachers. I show, however, that the reforms result in outcomes that contradict the claims of the reform proponents. The tests are not as objective as proposed, student learning has not improved, and academic inequality has not decreased at the rate equal to that before the reforms (Hursh, 2005a, 2006; Lee, 2006).

In chapter 6, Pauline Lipman and I examine Chicago's recent educational and social reforms as an example of "actually existing neoliberalism" (Brenner

& Theodore, 2002). Chicago's reforms, in particular Renaissance 2010, have increased corporate control over schools and developed a dual school system in which the already advantaged white middle-class students increase their advantages over working-class students. Furthermore, Renaissance 2010 remakes not only public schools but also the city itself. Renaissance 2010 is part of a larger project to raze low-income African American communities with the goal of gentrifying areas with new condominiums, luxury apartments, and retail services. As such, Renaissance 2010 serves as an example of how neoliberal education and economic policies are implemented as the way to position Chicago as a global city central to the financial, real estate, retail, and service industries, and how such efforts are also being resisted (see Lipman & Haines, 2007).

Finally, in chapter 7, I suggest what we might do to counter neoliberal education and social policies. Poet and essayist Adrienne Rich (2001) writes that we have two choices:

> One is the development of a literate, articulate, and well-informed citizenry so that the democratic process can continue to evolve and the promise of radical equality can be brought to closer realization. The other is the perpetuation of a class system dividing an elite, nominally "gifted" few, tracked from an earlier age, from a very large underclass essentially to be written off as alienated from language and science, from poetry and politics, from history and hope—toward low-wage temporary jobs. The second is the direction our society has taken. The results are devastating in terms of the betrayal of a generation of youth. The loss to the whole of society is incalculable. (p. 162)

I begin the chapter by showing how neoliberals hijack globalization to argue that we have no choice other than to adopt neoliberal policies (and neoliberalism is supposedly about choice!). For example, Thomas Friedman endlessly promotes neoliberalism as both desirable and inevitable in his best-selling books, including *The World Is Flat: A Brief History of the Twenty-first Century* (2005) and *The Lexus and the Olive Tree* (1999). He argues: "The driving force behind globalization is free-market capitalism—the more you let market forces rule and the more you open your economy to free trade and competition, the more efficient your economy will be" (1999, p. 9). George W. Bush asserts that NCLB is necessary because we live in a global world in which we must compete with China and India (U.S. Department of Education, 2006b, p. 2). According to neoliberals, we have no alternative.

However, I provide just some of the data revealing that neoliberalism's accomplishments fall short of its claims. It has both failed to increase economic growth and to decrease economic inequality within and between countries. Furthermore, by always focusing on economic growth and profit, it has exacerbated other problems, such as global warming, and undermined both human health and the health of the environment. Highlighting neoliberalism's failures and contradictions suggests possibilities for repealing neoliberal economic and education policies (Hursh, 2006, 2007b).

I then specifically turn to what we might do to repeal recent neoliberal education policies. Michael Apple, in *Educating the "Right" Way: Markets, Standards, God and Inequality* (2001), asserts that we need a forward-looking, strategic alternative to neoliberal governance and teacher de-skilling (p. 97). I suggest that we need to continue to create classrooms where students are active, critical participants in the world and make public how such efforts are undermined by current policies. We must become politically engaged in changing education policies. It is not enough to work in our own classrooms and schools; we must educate the public about the purposes of democratic schooling and the harm that the recent reforms have caused to those goals.

Of course, progressive approaches to education, such as what I describe, are made ever more difficult by the increasing emphasis on standardized testing. I argue, therefore, that if we are to have democratic schools we need to have a socially democratic, rather than a neoliberal, society. I conclude by suggesting ways in which educators might be part of a new social movement to transform the United States and take back our communities and schools. In making this argument I draw on my own experiences working for progressive educational reform in New York and elsewhere.

NOTE

1. A 15-minute video clip on the Urban Academy is presented near the end of the third-volume of *Only a Teacher*, produced and directed by Claudia Levin, Princeton, NJ: Films for the Humanities & Sciences (2001). The video *Looking for an Argument: An Inquiry Course at Urban Academy Laboratory High School*, Avram Barlow, is available from Teachers College Press (2004).

2

Demystifying Education: Theorizing Practice and Practicing Theory

I think I'm in a fair way to become an educational crank. I sometimes think I will drop teaching phil[osophy] directly, and teach it via pedagogy.

—*John Dewey*

Not only had I never planned on being a teacher, I had not really planned on going to university. Further, given that neither of my parents finished high school, my twin brother and I were the oldest of four children, and I had no relatives attending college, I was unfamiliar with choosing a university, applying for admission, and navigating university life. After barely surviving my first two years in university, I began not only to succeed but also to reflect on my difficulties and successes. I wanted to understand how I, a working-class male more interested in sports than school, managed to become interested in school and the world of ideas. Therefore, critiquing my own public school and university experience became my first effort at critically analyzing the educational system. I describe some of those experiences here not because I think my experiences are exceptional. Rather, they help us understand how education can both reproduce and challenge the status quo and inequalities.

I had not thought about education as an issue worth pursuing until my junior year in college. But during that year I began to reflect on my own and others' educational experiences at three different levels. The first level focused on my experience as a working-class boy who overcame numerous barriers to become moderately academically successful. These reflections led me to contemplate (what I now understand) how the mismatch between working-class students' cultural and social capital and that of educational institutions (Bourdieu, 1986) undermines working-class students' academic success but facilitates upper- and middle-class students' academic success. Therefore, while the educational process appears to be objective and fair, in fact, upper-class and middle-class students are more likely to succeed not because of their greater inherent academic ability or effort, but because their cultural experiences (or cultural capital) match those of educational institutions. Furthermore, because upper- and middle-class students are likely to know someone who has successfully navigated the system of higher education, they are more likely to succeed. I was beginning to question whether education really rewarded students based on their academic ability.

The second kind of analysis came about because of the larger political context in which schools and universities existed. At the time, students across the country were questioning the Vietnam War, joining the civil rights movement, and fighting to make their universities more relevant. I began to question why particular issues were ignored and began to organize with other students and faculty teach-ins on the Vietnam War and to push for courses in what we called black history and women's studies.

The last and third kind of analysis focused on creating alternative educational institutions and pedagogies. I began working with an alternative university that offered free courses taught by area residents (including university faculty, high school and university students, and townspeople) to anyone who enrolled. This alternative university—then given, unfortunately, the sexist name of University for Man and presently called only by its acronym, UFM—promoted courses focusing on subjects neglected by the traditional university. During the three years in which I worked at UFM, courses focused on topics such as the civil rights movement, the world in the year 2000, art and creativity, and social change. On two occasions I taught a course on existential philosophy using several books as readings, including Maxine Greene's *Existential Encounters for Teachers* (1967).

GROWING UP WORKING CLASS, ENTERING THE
MIDDLE CLASS, AND CRITIQUING THE STATUS QUO

In 1948, I was born, along wih my twin brother, into the baby boom generation and a working-class family. Neither my father nor my mother graduated from high school. Moreover, my father was underage when he enlisted in the Navy near the end of World War II to escape some difficulties. After his time in the Navy, my father was a construction worker and later an owner-operator of a small construction company (I sometimes worked for him for a dollar a day). My mother worked at home until my father died at the age of forty-two, after which she worked in factories, grocery stores, and restaurants. Now, more than thirty-five years later, she still works several days a week.

My early educational experiences were not auspicious. Family mythology has it that my twin brother and I failed kindergarten—I suspect in large part because we were inordinately shy—but were passed on to first grade because our teachers didn't want to teach us for another year. I did poorly in school until the end of second grade when my mother, in response to my query regarding how to add all the numbers on the grocery receipt, did not tell me to wait until my teacher taught me how to "carry" in addition. Instead, in a few minutes, she taught me. The mystery of schooling was broken; knowledge for the first time seemed not to be something possessed only by experts. Learning was no longer inherently difficult. Subsequently, with my new skill and confidence, I became a math whiz and did better in third grade. However, as an elementary and secondary student I rarely felt comfortable in the classroom. Neither the goals, nor rules, nor reasons were clear to me, and I usually aimed to just get through the day without being embarrassed or punished.

While school was becoming tolerable, life outside of school proved to be equally challenging. In the early years, we moved in and around New York City but in 1954 we settled in Levittown, New York, the archetypal postwar suburb. Levittown had no residents of color. First, as Ira Katznelson documents in *When Affirmative Action Was White: The Untold Story of Racial Inequality in the Twentieth Century* (2005), black vets were far less likely to obtain mortgages under the G.I. Bill than white soldiers. But, even if black vets could obtain mortgages, Levitt, the developer, sold his homes to only whites and had buyers sign a covenant that they would only resell to whites, a practice finally eliminated as illegal in 1968 (Brodkin, 2001). Levittown, presently a middle-class community, was initially a blue-collar community of *white* World War II veterans working their way up in the world. It was soon after moving to Levittown that I was first challenged by what it means to grow up a working-class male.

Levittown homes were filled with young families and, when school was not in session, boys filled the streets playing games. The first test of masculinity came as the neighborhood boys chose sides for the daily stickball (and later touch football) game. Not only had I not played baseball before but, as twins, my brother and I were also the smallest and weakest boys of the bunch. We were chosen last with the complaint "do we hafta take him?"—a pattern that was to hold for several years. In response, we were determined not to be chosen last but to be one of the prized players chosen early. The desire to become a better athlete, along with my lack of confidence regarding schooling, led me to prefer athletics to academics.

On reflection, choosing athletics over academics had several advantages. While I never quite understood what it took to succeed in school, sports gave me a place in which I understood quite literally the "game" and knew what it would take to do well. Sports have often been an area in which boys find rewards not found in schools. A survey of thirteen- to eighteen-year-old Australian boys revealed that sports offered them:

> [The] possibility of pursuing their own standards of excellence in ways they felt they had some control over. . . . For many, playing sports was in a sense losing oneself into the sport completely. For that time, all needs were being satisfied: physical, mental, social and emotional. All other problems and life pleasures ceased to exist: being blocked out by this total involvement in sport. There was a sense of urgency and need to have this escape. It is an escape which they feel frees them to be truly themselves, and at their best. (Gilbert & Gilbert, 1998, p. 60)

Although I loved sports, I could not go out for sports in high school because I delivered afternoon papers in order to earn money for personal belongings and the books I came to love. Consequently, I only went out for high school athletics my senior year, and that was in track and cross-country, which did not require the previous experience of team sports like football, my real passion. However, I played daily in the streets and left Levittown after high school knowing that I had reached my goal: rather than being the last player picked, I was more often the first.

Around the age of eight or nine I discovered books. Books were, in part, an escape from a world that was physically and emotionally dangerous: older and stronger boys and impenetrable social and school rules. Books also gave me access to a world beyond school and the streets. I began reading extensively, some might say excessively. At home I collected my own library of paperback books, reading, among others, the novels of Aldous Huxley, Sinclair Lewis, George Orwell, William Golding, J. D. Salinger, Ian Fleming; mysteries by Agatha Christie; and science fiction by Edgar Rice Burroughs and Ray Bradbury, while barely keeping up with required class readings. I often felt, as did Mark Twain, that "schooling was getting in the way of my education." However, because reading was not something working-class boys talked about, I never revealed my interest in books to my teachers and only to a few of my friends.

Further, my writing skills were deplorable. In seventh grade, I continually failed the weekly spelling test, resulting in numerous detentions meant to prod me to study. In twelfth grade, I managed to write a four-page essay that was one long incoherent paragraph. And while I read novels on my own, in English class the answers to teachers' questions about what we read seemed to me too subjective, therefore posing too much of a risk for me to raise my hand and answer. While I usually managed a "C" in English, I failed one quarter.

In contrast, math and science were not only perceived as masculine subjects, they were easier because they had clear objective answers that could be determined using the proper procedure. Math and science, then, were the subjects in which I excelled.

Upon entering high school, I "chose" the vocational track. "Chose" is within quotes because I was neither aware of the other choices nor what purposes tracking served. Nor can I claim to have actively planned my escape from the vocational to the honors track. In the spring of my freshman year, a school administrator announced in the boys' study hall (we were divided by sex for study hall and gym) that a test (an IQ test, I later learned) would be given to those interested in majoring in architecture or electrical or mechanical engineering. Since the study hall teachers were prone to giving detention to the boys en masse and I detested detentions that kept me from getting home to play sports, taking the test seemed the safer of the two choices. I achieved the required score for admission (benefiting from the gender and race bias of IQ tests, the reality that in the early 1960s few girls applied for architecture or engineering programs, and my math ability and years of secretly reading), and I began tenth grade majoring in architecture. At the same time, although I did not realize it until my high school reunion thirty years later, I was also admitted to the honors program.

Entering the architecture program benefited me more in terms of what I was to gain from other students about applying for university than what I learned about architecture. During my senior year *all* of my architecture classmates applied for university. They advised me regarding where I might apply and I sent away for applications. But when I received the applications, I did not know—because I had never talked with anyone who had a baccalaureate degree—whether to fill out the application for undergraduate school or, because I was a high school graduate, to apply for graduate school. I decided to fill out the front of the applications, applied for undergraduate school, was admitted and, because I had no way to evaluate programs, decided on Kansas State University, 1,500 miles from New York City.

Before heading west, I had to earn money to help pay for college. In the summer between high school and university, I began my first full-time job working with my brother in a factory assembling pool tables. It was in that and a subsequent factory that I first encountered race as an issue. In both factories salaried management were white and hourly workers were almost all black or Puerto Rican. My brother and I became friends with the hourly workers, socializing with them outside of work. As a factory worker, I saw myself as no more intelligent than the other blue-collar workers. However, I was privileged because, as a white university student, the routine and demeaning factory work were only temporary. In school and at work I became aware of class distinctions. In school, middle-class students were knowledgeable of postsecondary education and had the cultural capital that I did not have. But in the factory, because I had the opportunity for a career, rather than just a job, I became middle class (Adams et al., 2000).

Further, attending university and doing so in Kansas heightened class and race as issues. First, because I was working class, I began university disadvantaged in comparison to most of the other students. For example, upon flying into Manhattan, Kansas, late at night, for the first time, I asked the taxi driver to drop me off at the return address printed on the envelope in which I was sent housing information. Never having been on a university campus nor having any knowledge of dormitories, I did not realize until after the taxi departed that I was dropped off in front of the administration building, now closed for the evening. Upon rereading my mail and asking for directions, I learned that my dorm was a quarter mile away. I struggled off dragging my luggage behind me.

Not only did I not understand university housing, I did not know how to obtain course textbooks. While students arrived in class with textbooks, I sat without. Because, at the time, the university bookstore did not sell textbooks and I had not found the bookstores off campus, it was only when I finally asked students where they purchased their books that I learned that the bookstores near campus sold course texts.

While I might have had the ability to initially succeed at university, my unfamiliarity with college culture undermined my efforts. I nearly failed my courses that first year. But I learned that success in college depended in part on not what you knew but how you presented yourself in class. I came to understand that academic and economic success depended on more than merit. During my college years I both gained the cultural and social capital (Bourdieu & Passeron, 1977) necessary to enter the middle class and, at the same time, began to critique middle-class culture.

Almost simultaneously with learning how to succeed in college, I began to question whether university success was desirable and why the curriculum embodied a consensual, middle-class, colonial view of the world. I became disillusioned with the university's silence regarding the Vietnam War and the civil rights movement (Fulbright, 1966). At the moment in which I was poised to enter the middle class, the countercultural critique of the middle class supported me in rejecting the middle class as consumerist and oppressive (Roszak, 1968). Lastly, in contrast to my summer experiences working in factories, I was astonished by the lack of students of color at the university. Few students of color attended the university, and those people of color who lived in the community lived literally on the other side of the tracks on the edge of town farthest from the university.

In the spring and summer of 1968, first Martin Luther King Jr. and then Bobby Kennedy were assassinated, and antiwar activists demonstrated at the Democratic National Convention in Chicago. While I was naïve about the civil rights movement, my experience working with minorities in factories enlightened me about class and racial oppression in the United States. Consequently, I was shocked when, upon King's death, some university students celebrated and shouted, "Hooray, the nigger is dead!" I was learning that racism existed and that the Chicago police would riot against demonstrators using their freedom of speech.

By the end of the summer, I had concluded that the United States was not "the best of all possible worlds" but was, in fact, a racist, classist, and sexist society. I was beginning to understand how my own working-class experience gave me an understanding of the world that differed from that of my middle-class peers. Furthermore, I realized that democracy in America was and continues to be at risk. Such a realization required that I begin to think through the characteristics of a democratic society and how we might nurture them. Then, and now, one of my central concerns was what appeared to be the increasing difficulty of questioning the status quo and imagining a better world. A diminished view of social change that focuses on technological improvement and the production and use of more commodities characterized the postwar period of the 1950s and early 1960s, as well as our present time. Moral and political considerations of equality and the quality of life were rarely raised.

Surmising that the beating and arrests of protesters at the Democratic National Convention indicated that those in power feared that the protesters might have a legitimate critique, I began to examine more closely the history, policies, and politics of the Vietnam War. Soon thereafter I was organizing anti-war protests and teach-ins on my own campus. Such activities led the Nixon administration to assign a second lieutenant from nearby Fort Riley to tail me throughout the day and report on my activities. The second lieutenant enrolled in the existential philosophy course that I taught at the alternative university and, after the last class, revealed that he was assigned to follow me, provided copies of his reports, and thanked me for an enjoyable experience.

While I hoped that the university might be more open to my political views than the Nixon administration, they were not. After the bombing of Cambodia, President Nixon, feeling that the conservative Midwest was a safe place to give his first campus speech, came to Kansas State University. The university and Secret Service prohibited signs critical of the president, allowing only pro-Nixon signs. When a friend and I held up a sign that read "*If you make peaceful evolution impossible you make violent revolution inevitable—John F. Kennedy,*" we were immediately seized by the Secret Service and removed from the building. Over the next few weeks the university and the state upped the ante, as both the university and the Republican candidate for governor threatened to have me arrested and expelled from the university. The Republican candidate lost but became Nixon's assistant attorney general and presided in 1973 over the disastrous confrontation at Wounded Knee. Meanwhile, the university backed off. I was following Senator Fulbright's advice, in *The Arro-*

gance of Power: "to criticize one's country is to do it a service and pay it a compliment. It is a service because it may spur the country to do better than it is doing; it is a compliment because it evidences a belief that that the country can do better than it is doing" (1966, p. 25). Clearly neither the government nor the university agreed.

Nixon's Vietnam War policies led me to examine how particular political views gained dominance and legitimacy over others. I soon realized that such questions are essentially social and philosophical and that we all are, to varying degrees, engaged in social and philosophical analysis. I began to take seriously C. Wright Mills's (1959) description of sociology as the work of the sociological imagination, which is the process through which we examine the larger structural forces that affect our lives and make sense of our experience as not idiosyncratic but societal. It is the way in which we come to understand our *personal troubles* as *public issues* (Lemert, 1997, p. 12).

Moreover, we are engaged in philosophical questions as we raise questions about the curriculum content and the organization of schools and classrooms. When we do so, we are raising philosophical questions regarding the nature of knowledge (epistemology), the purposes of schooling and life (values), and the relations among individuals in schools (ethics). And, as in sociology, as we do so, we connect the personal and the public. Maxine Greene, whose book *Existential Encounters for Teachers* (1967) was my introduction to educational philosophy, understands the relationship between the personal and the public. She begins *The Dialectic of Freedom* (1988) with this description:

> This book arises out of a lifetime's preoccupation with quest, with pursuit. On the one hand, the quest has been deeply *personal*: that of a woman striving to affirm the feminine as wife, mother, and friend, while reaching, always reaching, beyond the limits imposed by the obligations of a woman's life. On the other hand, it has been in some sense deeply *public* as well: that of a person struggling to connect the undertaking of education, with which she has been so long involved, to the making and remaking of a public space, a space of dialogue and possibility. (p. xi)

Greene, as a philosopher, educator, and woman, both acknowledges the limits placed on her and us and aims to reach beyond them. She wants to rethink and reshape what we know, do, and value. "What I am describing here is a mode of utopian thinking: thinking that refuses mere compliance, that looks down roads not yet taken to the shapes of a more fulfilling social order, to more vibrant ways of being in the world" (Greene, 1995, p. 5). She resists merely complying with the current social order and instead engages in utopian thinking that hopefully will lead to a better life for her and others in society.

In thinking through what I want to do as an educator and a citizen, I have tried to understand why people comply and submit to social conditions that limit their own and others' understanding and growth and the difficulties we face in proposing "utopian" alternative futures. Furthermore, I have understood the plight of the individual and society as intertwined so that individual growth necessitates social institutions and structures that support that growth. In order to understand how society might support learning, it is necessary to understand what schools do and can do. For me, making sense of how we live and learn required becoming an educator.

Noting how Mills and Greene linked their own personal problems with public issues, I reflected on how formal education rarely helps people make those connections. As a sophomore I read Paul Goodman's books, *Growing Up Absurd* (1960) and *Compulsory Miseducation* (1964), in which he criticized education for preparing students to fit into society and the workplace rather than to critique and reform it. Goodman (1964) denounced the educational system for not providing students with skills to analyze and change the world but, instead, "guaranteeing the right character" (p. 21). It is in schools, he wrote, that

> our citizens learn that life is inevitably routine, depersonalized, venally graded; that it is best to toe the mark and shut up; that there is no place for spontaneity, open sexuality, free spirit. Trained in the school, they go on to the same quality of jobs, culture, politics. This is education, mis-education, socializing to the national norms and regimenting to the national "needs." (p. 23)

Goodman echoed Dewey's (1915) criticism that education focused on the needs of business and provided narrow job training in the vocational track and the narrow academic focus in the college-prep track (Weltman, 2000). Goodman (1964) criticized the then–New York commissioner of education for stating: "The educational role is, by and large, to provide—at public and parents' expense—apprentice-training for corporations, government, and the teaching professions itself. And also to train the young to handle constructively their problems of adjustment to authority" (p. 18). Goodman (1960) detested the idea that education should be preparation for the needs of corporations and government, for fitting "people wherever they are needed in the production system" (p. 4).

Goodman (1962) argued that the emphasis on meeting the needs of the bureaucracy caused many of our difficulties with adolescents. Schools offered adolescents few "worthwhile experiences." Further, he deplored the postwar culture of production and consumption that "dried up the spontaneous imagination of ends and the capacity to invent ingenious expedients" that "disintegrated communities" and "destroyed human scale" (p. 10). Such acceptance made it difficult to offer proposals to change schools and society. Consequently, he felt it was increasingly difficult to propose alternatives: "The structures and folkways of our society are absurd, but [most people feel] they can no longer be changed. Any hint of changing them disturbs our resignation and rouses anxiety" (p. 6).

Educational institutions rarely assist and mostly undermine our ability to connect our personal or private troubles and the larger social structure. This is, as I have argued elsewhere (Hursh, 2003), because modern capitalist society assumes a consensus has emerged around valuing economic production and consumption over everything else, linked with instrumental rationality.

Yet Goodman was not quite so pessimistic in other publications. In *Utopian Essays and Practical Proposals* (1962), he urged us to create alternative visions of the future. Similarly, Greene calls for a space of dialogue and possibility. Realizing that it is not enough to critique social inequities but to change them (Marx, 1932), I took seriously Goodman's proposal that we develop communities and educational institutions that would connect the personal with the public and provide spaces for democratic dialogue. Further, as a working-class male still more comfortable with things than ideas, I found more reward in creating institutions and working alongside others than in theorizing possibilities.

During my junior year, I volunteered to assist at the alternative university, UFM, and at the beginning of my senior year I was hired as the assistant director and worked there for the next three years. Besides offering semester-long courses, the other two staff members and I organized national conferences on developing similar postsecondary alternatives and on progressive school reform. For the latter, we recruited as presenters noted progressive educational reformers such as Jonathan Kozol (1967, 1972), George Dennison (1969), and John Holt (1964, 1969). I immersed myself in the educational reform literature of the time and began writing articles and speaking out on developing democratic schools.

My educational reform goals reflected my own class experiences. For me, how one succeeds in education had gradually become demystified. When my mother taught me how to "carry" in math, I realized that learning did not have to be difficult. Upon reading, interpreting, and applying the ideas of Fulbright, Goodman, Greene, and others, I gained the confidence to believe that the sense I made of readings was valid. I began to think about how to transform schools into spaces in which students and teachers together ask questions about what is worth knowing and how we should learn. I wanted to explore how schools might be democratically organized to respect the experience of adults and the interests of students. It was no longer enough to talk about reforming schools: It was time to create new ones.

Therefore, I left UFM to begin an eight-year career (1972–1980) as an elementary teacher and director of two different private alternative schools. I began at The New School, Omaha, Nebraska, as a teacher's aide, became a full-time teacher a few weeks later, became head teacher-director during my second year, and left after three years to start my own school, The Living Learning School, in Manhattan, Kansas. I taught there for five and one-half years.

LINKING PERSONAL TROUBLES TO PUBLIC PROBLEMS: DEVELOPING DEMOCRATIC SCHOOLS AND SPACES

Situating my own personal troubles within larger historical and social structures led me to understand that my own personal decisions were limited by and affected the larger social and political context. Therefore, if schools are to create the kinds of critical, reflective citizens that both Dewey and I hoped for, educators need to understand the larger social and historical context and realize that everything about educational goals and processes are both contested and political.

By *political* I do not necessarily mean (but do not exclude) politics as related to political representation but political, as described by Zygmunt Bauman (1999), in the sense of the "ability to imagine a better world and to do something to make it better" (p. 1). Or, as author and poet Adrienne Rich (1993) eloquently describes:

> The moment when a feeling enters the body—is political. This touch is political. By which I mean, that *politics* is the effort to find ways of humanely dealing with each other—as groups and as individuals—politics being simply process, the breaking down of barriers of oppression, tradition, culture, ignorance, fear, self-protectiveness. (p. 24, emphasis in original)

By calling for linking personal problems with social structures and engaging in ways to humanely deal with one another, I am also calling for a rebirth of the public sphere in which lively debate and discussion occurs regarding the purposes of society and schooling. Bauman (2000) laments what he describes as the demise of public issues in public spaces (p. 40) and, consequently, "What is wrong with the kind of society we live in is that it stopped questioning itself. We are more critical but our critique is more toothless, unable to affect the agenda set for our 'life-political' choices" (p. 22).

Under our current neoliberal policies, economic growth and efficiency have become the means by which we measure all things. Schools exist, by that rationale, to produce workers and consumers. Everything and everyone is for sale. Citizenship is reduced to consumption. The only form of citizenship that government and the markets tolerate is the "consumerist one." What is left for the individual is the goal of accumulating "junk and more junk" (Baumann, 1999, p. 5). As I will later discuss, under policies such as No Child Left Behind, students and parents are no longer members of a school community, but instead are individual consumers shopping for the best school. Schools, too, have been reduced to places in which economic production and consumption is emphasized.

In contrast, I call for a citizenship and an educational system that questions the increasing commodification of everything. Rather than measuring education only in terms of what it contributes to our economic system, I focus on what education contributes to our developing a coherent vision of a democratic society and enabling teachers and students to work toward it. Furthermore, I argue that the emphasis on markets and choice undermines public debate and what Young (2000) and Gutmann and Thompson (2004) describe as deliberative democracy.

It is then, in education, where the perennial social and philosophical questions regarding how we live in the world are put into practice. It is in teaching that we can raise questions about which knowledge is worth knowing and how to learn. In thinking about teaching, I had become familiar with the writing and teaching of reformers such as Maxine Greene (1967), Jonathan Kozol (1967, 1972), Herb Kohl (1967, 1969), George Dennison (1969), and others. But it was John Dewey, not surprising given that he remains the most well-known American philosopher and educator, whose writing and life most influenced me. It was Dewey who concluded in the late 1800s that the only way for him to sort though his philosophical and social understanding of society was to become an educator and start his own school.

JOHN DEWEY: USING PEDAGOGY TO UNDERSTAND PHILOSOPHY

When Dewey arrived at the University of Chicago in 1894, his primary focus had been philosophy and psychology. But in Chicago he became immersed in the theory and practice of social reform. His influences included fellow faculty at the University of Chicago, including Albion Small, one of a small group of sociologists who argued that social inequality was not inevitable but was a consequence of unequal social structures (Menand, 2001). For Small, and other emerging critics of the way in which society perpetuated social inequality through uneven life chances, inequality could be reduced through social change, particularly education. Small (1896), particularly for a sociologist, was overly optimistic regarding the power of teachers and education, stating that "educators shall not rate themselves as leaders of students, but as makers of society. Sociology knows of no means for the amelioration or reform of society more radical than those of which teachers hold the leverage" (p. 184).

Dewey was influenced not only by his university colleagues, but also by social reformers such as Jane Addams, the founder of Hull House. Hull House is commonly described as a settlement house but in practice it was an educational institution that sponsored classes, lectures, clubs, a daycare, nursery, and kindergarten (Menand, 2001). Dewey's friendship with Addams, Small, and other social reformers contributed to Dewey's decision to begin a school. At the moment he decided to start a school, he shared that decision in a letter to his wife Alice—a letter that reveals a passion that Dewey often felt but omitted from his theoretical writings:

I think I'm in a fair way to become an educational crank. I sometimes think I will drop teaching phil [philosophy]—directly, & teach it via pedagogy. When you think of the thousands & thousands of young 'uns who are practically being ruined negatively if not positively in the Chicago schools every year, it is enough to make you go out & howl on the street corners like the Salvation Army. There is an image of a school growing up in my mind all the time; a school where some actual & literal constructive activity shall be the centre & source of the whole thing. . . . The school is the one form of social life which is abstracted & under control—which is directly experimental, and if philosophy is ever to be an experimental science, the construction of a school is its starting point. (Dewey, 1894, as cited in Menand, 2001, p. 319–320)

Dewey's vision of a school as a form of social life opened at the University of Chicago in January 1896 as the University Elementary School, a school that everyone knew as the Dewey School. Dewey, who also taught courses in psychology, conceived of the school as neither a teacher education institution nor as a psychology laboratory, but as "a *philosophy* laboratory" (Menand, 2001, p. 322, italics added). For Dewey, knowledge was inseparably united with doing. Louis Menand (2001) writes, "education at the Dewey School was based on the idea that knowledge is a byproduct of activity: people do things in the world, and the doing results in learning something that, if deemed useful, gets carried along into the next activity" (p. 322).

Since, for Dewey, all activity should be educational and transformative, schools were not to be the only educational institutions, all institutions, including ones in which we worked, should be educational. Such views led him to vehemently disagree with the dominant idea that education should be preparation for work and that workers would be evaluated based on their efficiency. He disagreed, for example, with David Snedden, who as commissioner of education in Massachusetts and a vocal educational reformer, aimed to incorporate into education ideas from the scientific efficiency movement.

Social efficiency began with the ideas of Frederick Winslow Taylor (1911; see also Kanigel, 2005), whose publications on "scientific management" promoted standardization, accountability, and rewards and punishments in the workplace. Snedden (1924) aspired to shape schools around what industrialists wanted students to know and do. But Dewey (1915), in a debate in the *New Republic,* fiercely disagreed with Snedden. Because the workplace did not sufficiently emphasize the welfare of the worker, Dewey argued against preparing students as workers for the "existing industrial regime" but rather for an educational system that "would alter the existing industrial system, and ultimately transform it" into a democratic institution (p. 42). Dewey identified the crucial issue that was to dominate education throughout the last century: Should education be preparation for work and the existing social order or for critical thinking that transformed the social order?

Like Dewey, I realized that it is in education that the perennial social and philosophical questions regarding how we live in the world are put into practice. It is in teaching that we can raise questions about which knowledge is most worth knowing and how we learn. We can investigate how to organize social institutions so as to develop the knowledge, skills, and attitudes necessary for democratic citizenship. I realized that I, too, might become "an educational crank." However, because I had not enrolled in a teacher education program, I was not a certified teacher and, therefore, I took a position as an assistant teacher in a private elementary school. The night before my first day teaching, I listed questions that I wanted to answer. At the time, I had only a vague idea of how the kind of school I desired might look. But from my own experience and the experience of others, particularly educational critics from the 1960s and 1970s (whose contributions to the last four decades of progressive reforms unfortunately have been slighted), I had some idea of my direction. My essential questions focused on the curriculum, the nature of student freedom and learning, the role of the authority, and the relationship between teachers and students and between students:

1. What is the nature of subjects in the curriculum? As I saw it, how we commonly think about school subjects had three weaknesses. First, educators inadequately acknowledge that in the process of teaching one subject area, we are often teaching others. For example, when we engage in any subject we are also teaching the language arts or the communication skills of reading, writing, speaking, and listening. Science typically includes not only language arts but also math. (This is precisely why current efforts in this high-stakes era to improve students' reading abilities by not teaching science and social studies are so misguided.)

In contrast to the traditional elementary curriculum, where the school day is divided into subject periods, the Dewey school focused on students learning through projects, such as cooking, making clothes, or building a "clubhouse" (in truth, a small one-story building). One graduate of the Dewey school, Dr. Tenney (for whom Tenney Park in Madison, Wisconsin, is named) could not recall, when later interviewed by educational historian Herbert Kliebard, any lessons specifically devoted to reading and writing.

Second, the distinction between subjects themselves is increasingly unclear. By attempting to keep the subjects distinct as separate fields we engage in what Postman and Weingartner labeled "the hardening of the categories" (1969, p. 80). Fortunately, progressive educators, from Dewey and Frances Parker at the beginning of the last century (Kliebard, 2004), through to Herb Kohl (1967, 1969) and others during the 1960s and 1970s, provide examples of how to develop holistic curriculum.

Third, we inadequately acknowledge the contested nature of the subjects themselves. The purpose and content of English and social studies or history have always been debated (Hursh & Ross, 2000). In developing the curriculum for history courses, one has to consider that the significance and meaning of events are open to multiple interpretations, as often are the "facts" themselves. To take what should be by now an obvious example, up until the last decade or so, Columbus has been generally described as "discovering" America. However, the quincentenary of his voyages promoted a reassessment of the social and ecological consequences of his "discovery." Consequently, we are now likely to debate whether it is better to describe Columbus as encountering the New World or, less neutrally, invading it. Furthermore, increasing emphasis is placed on telling the story of those who are often excluded from the traditional Columbus narratives: the indigenous people of the Americas.

2. Early in *Education and Experience* (1963) Dewey raised the question: "What does freedom mean and what are the conditions under which it is capable of realization?" (p. 22). Then, as in the 1960s and 1970s, some progressive educators aspired to free students of the constraints students experienced in more traditional schools. As a new teacher I posed the question: "How much freedom should we allow students?" thinking, like some progressive educators before me, that our educational problems might be solved if we just gave students freedom to learn. However, in time, I learned that the issue of freedom could be elusive and misleading. Dewey argued: "There can be no greater mistake . . . than to treat such freedom as an end in itself" (p. 63). He did not conceive of freedom as the ability to do whatever one pleases but, instead, as action within the continuum of experience.

George Dennison, whose description of teaching and learning in *The Lives of Children: The Story of the First Street School* (1969) expands on Dewey's ideas regarding the relationship between freedom and activity, wrote:

> Freedom is not motion in a vacuum, but motion in a continuum. If we want to know what freedom is, we must discover what the continuum is. "The principle," Dewey remarks, "is not what justifies an activity." We might say something similar about freedom: it is another name for the fullness and final shape of activities. We experience the activities, not the freedom. (p. 4)

For Dewey and Dennison what was important for students was not to do whatever they wanted but to engage in whole meaningful activities. In traditional schools students experience the day as a series of unrelated activities in which they have little input into either the content or duration. But it is not desirable to simply hand the day over to the students. Rather, the question becomes how to arrange the school day so that students engage in and complete meaningful activities (Dennison, 1969, p. 4). How do we develop schools and classrooms in which students experience the continuity of learning?

The question is not an easy one to answer for it requires that we develop criteria for ending one activity and beginning another. It also leads to asking: How do we balance the need to follow through and build on previous learning while allowing for the possibility of changing directions and beginning anew? How do we organize the classroom so students can differ from one another in how much time and effort they give to an activity? And, finally, how do we understand continuity in schools?

3. How do students learn? In particular, how is schooling presently organized so that it undermines students' learning and how do we organize it to promote critical thinking? My experience as a critic of the Vietnam War was that many citizens were reluctant to question the government's policies and programs. During one of my appearances on a radio talk show, one caller stated that the public had no basis for questioning Nixon's bombing of Cambodia because the public has less knowledge than the administration. Such a stance ignores the possibility that governments everywhere present information in a way to suit their policies and that beyond the facts themselves all policies can be questioned regarding their intent and fairness. Hearing such

adult acquiescence led me to reflect on whether our school experiences pre-pared us to question the status quo.

As Paul Goodman (1964) describes, what students learn in school is to sub-mit themselves to routine, "to toe the mark and shut up; that there is no place for spontaneity" (p. 23). Students learn to fit in, and after succeeding at that, expect the same in jobs, culture, and politics. John Holt, in *How Children Fail* (1964), describes classroom practices in which students, rather than learning as part of the process of making sense of the world, store up facts to give back to the teacher. Teachers and students play the implicit game of "guess what the teacher is thinking," in which students try to guess the answer the teacher wants not by thinking so much as by listening for verbal clues. In contrast, Dennison (1969) summarizes learning as part of a collaborative process be-tween the teacher and student.

> There is no such thing as learning except (as Dewey tells us) in the continuum of experience. But this one continuum cannot survive in the classroom unless there is reality of encounter between the adults and the students. The teachers must be themselves, and not play roles. They must teach the students and not teach "subjects." The student, after all, is avid to acquire what he takes to be the necessities of life, and the teacher must not answer them with mere profession-alism and gimmickry. (p. 74)

For Dennison, Dewey, Holt, and Goodman, learning requires developing a re-lationship between adults and students and together making sense of the world.

4. What is the role of the adult in the classroom? What is the nature of adult authority? How we think about this question parallels the previous questions. In reflecting on how we think about the relationship between teachers and students, we err when we assume that teachers must choose between asserting or withholding their authority. When teachers continually assert their author-ity, therefore tightly controlling the classroom experience, students grow to mistrust their own experience and are anxious to please adults. But if in giv-ing students "freedom" teachers withhold their authority, then students are also likely to be anxious as they make decisions without adult guidance.

Again, Dewey is helpful in clarifying how we think about authority in schools. In desiring schools to be democratic institutions, Dewey wanted to eliminate coercion as much as possible. However, he warned against adults adopting the other extreme of rejecting their role as authorities. Dewey (1963) cautioned:

> Because the older [traditional] education imposes the knowledge, methods, and the rules of conduct of the mature person on the young, it does not follow, except on the basis of the extreme Either-Or philosophy, that the knowledge and skill of the mature person has no directive value for the experience of the immature.... [Rather, the] greater maturity of experience which should belong to the adult as educator puts him in a position to evaluate such experience of the young in a way in which the one having the less mature experience cannot do. It is then the business of the educator to see in what direction an experience is heading. There is no point in his being more mature if, instead of using his greater insight to help organize the conditions of the experience of the immature, he throws away his insight. The mature person, to put it in moral terms, has no right to withhold from the young on given occasions whatever capacity for sympathetic understanding his own experiences has given him. (pp. 21–22, 38)

5. In the classroom, what should be the relationship between student and student? In the traditional classroom, knowledge is passed from the teacher or textbook to the student. But if we envision schools as democratic communities in which students take responsibility for themselves and the wider community, what is the role of students in one another's learning? How might we begin to build on students' experiences and knowledge? How might students and adults learn from other students?

Of course, none of these questions can be answered definitively, but only tentatively, leading to revision and new questions. As a teacher, I can only answer them for today, for this lesson. Like Maxine Greene, who is nearing her nineties and describes herself as always evolving toward a future conception of herself, as "I am . . . not yet" (1998), teaching always evolves. I hope to provide insights from my own teaching that should help readers think through their own questions. I cannot offer "the one best way" (Tyack, 1974). Teaching is too complicated a process and dependent too much on the particular knowledge, interests, and abilities to respond to a particular method. From the beginning, I agreed with thoughtful observers such as Allen Graubard (1972), who wrote: "A point worth making is that education is not the sort of problem amenable to a sudden, new discovery, either of theory or of technique" (p. 32).

These are the questions with which I began as an elementary teacher and continue to use today. As a university professor, I struggle with how to encourage students to form their own questions and develop learning activities that are meaningful to them. I try to teach in ways that build on the students' experiences in schools, whether as university students, neophyte or experienced teachers, or administrators. At the same time, I remind myself that my thirty-five years of teaching and conducting research provides me with experience and knowledge that is helpful to students. And, I am still learning.

3

Years of Struggle and Hope

After three years of codirecting an alternative university, reading and writing about education, and visiting innovative schools, I began an eight-year career (1972–1980) as an elementary teacher in two different schools: the first, The New School in Omaha, Nebraska; and the second, The Living Learning School in Manhattan, Kansas, which I established. The story of my teaching and of those schools is not one of immediate and overwhelming success. Rather, what I hope to illuminate are some lessons regarding the nature of freedom and adult authority, the role students play in decision making, and the relationship between curriculum content and learning.

Before proceeding, some information regarding the schools themselves is necessary. Both schools were private parent-teacher governed schools. The New School was founded by parents and enrolled an average of seventy kindergarten through seventh grade students during the three years in which I taught there, the last two of which I also served as head teacher. After leaving The New School, I established The Living Learning School. Besides teaching, I also served as director of the school most of the five years in which I taught. On average, we enrolled thirty students from kindergarten through fourth grade. In both schools, students were not assigned to a grade level, but engaged in activities based on their interests and abilities.

Three points should be made. First, some may dismiss as irrelevant observations and lessons learned from teaching in two small private schools. However, over the last twenty years numerous small public schools have begun and many serve as models for the "small schools movement"—see the special issue of *Rethinking Schools* (2005, Summer). For example, two small New York City public schools, the Urban Academy (Cook, 2005; Barlowe & Mack, 2002) and Central Park East (Meier, 1995), have a similar student–teacher ratio to my own schools and Rose (1995) describes numerous innovative successful small schools in *Possible Lives: The Promise of Public Education in America.* Schools, such as the School Without Walls in Rochester, New York, and the Urban Academy, demonstrate how much we have learned about creating schools where teachers and students engage in meaningful teaching and learning.

Second, while I no longer direct a school or teach full time in an elementary classroom, I continue to learn from the preservice and practicing teachers that I regularly observe. For example, Aggie Seneway, a now retired elementary teacher whom I have observed and written with (Hursh & Seneway, 1998, 2001), structured her classroom so that students had input into decisions about what and how they would learn. I have also benefited from observing other teachers, both in the Rochester area and in New York City. Furthermore, I am involved in several projects developing and implementing innovative curriculum and pedagogy in schools, most recently with the goal of students learning about the relationship between the environment and human health and environmental sustainability. I continue to reflect on and change my teaching based on observations and conversations with master teachers.

Third, as I considered becoming a teacher, I questioned whether I should teach in private or public schools. At that time and in the conservative and largely rural Midwest, the prospects of finding a public school where I might have some control over what and how I taught seemed bleak. If I were living in some other community—such as Minneapolis and Chicago—I might have made another choice. But given that my goal was, like Dewey, to develop a school that supported a community of learners, the choices I made seemed sensible.

THE NEW SCHOOL: LEARNING FROM MISSTEPS

Armed with my thoughts on education but with no experience teaching at the elementary level, I began my teaching career in September 1972 at a private school in Omaha, Nebraska. The school had just opened with three full-time teachers, all of whom were relative neophytes. Two teachers, including the teacher-director, had taught for a few years, and the third had just completed student teaching. I was hired *after* the first week of school as a part-time, temporary aide to the science and art teacher. After one week, I became the permanent full-time science and art teacher. During the second year, the board chose me to replace the founding teacher-director, and I held that position until resigning after the third year.

In the same year that the school began, Allen Graubard's (1972) *Free the Children: Radical Reform and the Free School Movement* was published. As a supporter of school reform, Graubard's aim was to not only raise questions about education and society in general, but also to raise questions about some of the prominent alternative school projects of the time, including Summerhill in England (see Neil's *Summerhill*, 1960; Snitzer, 1964; Ayers, 2003). Graubard (1972) desired "to be as clear as possible about the serious problems that exist in these schools in theory and practice, and . . . to analyze where these problems come from and how they might best be understood and confronted" (p. xi).

Given the lack of successful models, designing a new school was not easy. How we answered the questions I raised at the end of the second chapter would be central to whether we succeeded. How would we think through the nature of the curriculum subjects, the continuity of learning, and the role of student choice, teacher authority, and other students in learning? The initial year indicated that we had a lot to learn. I begin this chapter by describing some of the problems in how the school day was initially organized, discuss the changes we made, and close the chapter describing a project from each of the two schools.

Because I joined the teaching staff after the first week, the organization of the school day was already in place. Organizational decisions were limited partly by the building in which the school was housed: a rustic seventy-year-old, two-story log building on a hillside in which the second floor was reserved for residential use. While rustic and charming, classrooms were limited to the four rooms below, three on the first floor, none of which opened directly to the others, and one in the basement that opened to the driveway.

Each of the four rooms was designated as a subject-area center with a teacher responsible for the room. The school day was divided into three periods—two before lunch and one after. At the beginning of each period and at the end of the day, students met in an assigned circle in one of the rooms. Each circle consisted of students from ages five to twelve. In the first circle of the day, each student shared what he or she had done the previous day, some vague ideas for that day, and anything else that seemed relevant.

For each period, teachers were allocated a set of cards on which was written one of the different subject areas that occurred in one of the rooms—science, social studies, math, language arts, and art. The number of cards for each subject area was limited so that no teacher would receive a disproportionate number of students. At the end of the meeting, students selected a card for the subject-area room to which they wanted to go. If all the cards were taken for a particular subject area, then a student would have to choose another.

From the present vantage point, the school's structure seems poorly thought out. However, the structure of the school day was guided by several ideals, all of which can be traced back to the beginnings of progressive education, most of which Dewey (1963) later criticized as misinterpretations of his thoughts. These ideals included promoting students' freedom of choice and control over their learning, reducing the teachers' role as authorities, and students interacting with and potentially learning from other students in the school community. While these may be positive ideals, the way in which they were implemented had significant negative consequences.

Often, in order to promote younger students benefiting from the experience of older students, progressive educators ended the practice of grouping students by age or grade, and instead grouped students across an age span of several years. However, having student discussion groups with students differing in age by up to nine years does not ensure students learning from one another: the differences in interests, concerns, and cognitive abilities made meaningful discussions difficult (I was just beginning to read Piaget, and Vygotsky was not yet published in the United States). Consequently, the circle discussions frustrated both teachers and students. Older students were frustrated by what they perceived as the immature issues raised by the youngest students and the younger students often could not understand the issues raised by older students.

Further, once the circles ended, students dispersed to the different rooms resulting in ten to fifteen students descending upon my room, usually ranging from five to fourteen years old. Students heading for math and language arts might responsibly expect that the teacher will hand them some math problems to do or have them read or write something at their ability level. But what were students to do in science and art? I did not advertise a project or unit, but was to respond to their interests. A few of the students had an idea of what they wanted to do; some arrived with no notion of what they wanted to do but would earnestly look for something. However, some came because they were following a friend, didn't want to do math or writing, or because they wanted to disrupt the work of other students. Some students would come to my room twice a day and some I would not see for weeks. I would try to get the students interested in activities and keep those whom I could not interest from disturbing others. In sum, it was a recipe for disaster characterized by chaos, frustration, and little learning.

As Dewey notes, our desire to provide students with freedom of choice ignores his argument that freedom is only meaningful as an activity in a continuum. Further, the expectation was that students would come to a room either knowing what they wanted to do or that the teacher would engage individual students in learning activities. In hindsight, the expectation that students could create their own activities was unrealistic. This implied that elementary students knew enough about science to develop a project (and that I had the resources readily available). Within these constraints, I moved about setting up materials for those ready to work, answering questions about science experiments or art projects, cajoling those who did not want to work, and giving ideas and listening to those who wanted to do something but were not sure what.

I think we made several mistakes in implementing our ideals. First, we misunderstood the nature of adult authority. Dewey would say that in our effort to refrain from using our authority "arbitrarily," we failed to use our "natural" authority. We felt that it was inappropriate to exert our greater experience as adults into the classroom context. This hesitancy to acknowledge and build on the greater experience of adults has, as Dewey notes in *Education and Experience* (1963), continually undermined progressive education efforts.

For example, John Holt, who authored numerous books critiquing traditional education and promoting progressive views, such as *How Children Learn* (1969) and *What Can I Do on Monday?* (1970), throughout his career became increasingly convinced that adults should play almost no role in directing or organizing student learning. In 1979, he visited my school and in response to one of my articles (Hursh, 1979) on teaching reading, he wrote:

> I think students would like to divide their lives between students' activities, things thought up and done by students for their own purposes; and adults' activities, things thought up and done by adults for their own purposes, with students taking part. But I am more and more troubled by the thought of adults thinking up things for students to do, no matter how creative. (Holt, personal communication, 1979)

He also suggested that schools model themselves after a Danish folk school he visited in which the adults and students did what they want and the teachers never suggest, however subtly or gently, what students do. While Holt criticized my teaching as too authoritative, my own assessment is that during the first year of teaching, we were not authoritative enough. There was no effective method of introducing projects or materials to students; students cannot be responsible for creating their own curriculum.

Indeed, if we reflect on how difficult it is for us as teachers to develop lessons and units without building on the ideas and experiences of other educators, how can we expect a seven-year-old to successfully do so? However, as teachers, as I will describe regarding the genesis of a geology unit, we can listen for students' questions and interests and develop learning activities in response.

Second, we mistakenly equated the positive ideal of treating every student as an individual with individualized instruction in which students individually determined what they were going to learn (choosing cards for a subject area) and how they were going to learn it (almost all students engaged in individual activities). This has been a persistent misunderstanding in progressive education. Respecting students as individuals does not require that students engage in individual, rather than group, activities. As Maxine Greene (1967) reminds us, "Dewey . . . warned that 'individualism' was destroying 'individuality'" (p. 15). In our effort to not duplicate what we felt were the failures of traditional schools, we dropped one extreme and adopted the other—we abrogated our authority and eliminated group activities.

Third, not only did we mistakenly promote student individualism, we did so within a traditional and limiting view of curriculum subjects and the school-day structure. We were responsible for different subject areas and made no effort to share with one another what we were teaching or to integrate them. Furthermore, because we divided the day into three time periods, students were expected to begin and end their activity within a predetermined time. Consequently, students worked on their own and, after finishing an activity, had to fill the time with additional activities or, if not completing the activity before the end of the period, would try to preserve the activity to return to it at another time. Students expressed resentment over the artificiality of the time periods and felt that it met the teachers' needs more than their own. The time periods did not meet our needs either but we had no idea how to organize the day differently.

All of this—the lack of integrated curriculum, adult guidance, and flexibility in scheduling—undermined students' continuity of learning. To quote Dennison (1969) again: "Freedom is not motion in a vacuum, but motion in a continuum. . . . Our concern for freedom is our concern for fulfillment—of activities we deem important and of persons we know are unique" (p. 4). Neither students nor teachers experienced fulfillment in what they were doing. Therefore, it was time for a change.

In revising the school structure, we had several specific goals: (1) To provide a method for adults to introduce learning activities to students and for those activities to continue, as appropriate, across days, weeks, or months. (2) To devise a way for students to responsibly plan their learning activities and for teachers to know who was doing what, when. (3) To make it possible for students to work with other students based on shared abilities or interests, regardless of age. (4) To ensure that students individually met every day with a teacher to plan their learning activities and evaluate their progress. (5) To enable students to meet with their peers to share how and what they were learning.

The new school structure (for both this and later The Living Learning School) had three major components: the "sign-up board," the advisor/advisee relationship, and the student log book. The faculty met at least once per week to discuss individual students' progress or lack thereof and to plan activities based on our learning goals and students' interests. We might plan to specifically focus on working with students on fractions using a variety of math manipulatives or review our progress in the architecture unit and plan for specific lessons during the upcoming week. These lessons might be posted on the sign-up board thus: "Architecture: this group will meet today and two additional times to build structures with different materials (for example, toothpicks and miniature marshmallows)."

Each morning, teachers, other adults, and students posted projects on the sign-up board for that and the next day, with several projects posted for every time period. Parents and other adults might offer a special project (we once hosted a world premiere of a professionally written children's play). Similarly, students might post that they were starting a newspaper or desired to discuss a novel or share their interest in military history. At the beginning of each school day, the students planned, in consultation with their advisor, both individual and group activities. As teachers, we then knew whom we would be working with and when.

Consequently, a student's typical day might begin with a group science activity, then reading a novel individually, playing basketball during recess, eating lunch while watching films, meeting with the architecture group planning a television show on city planning (more about that later), and conclude by working on math with a teacher available for assistance. By writing out their activities for each day, students committed themselves to specific activities, rather than, as previously, to a room. The amount of time committed to an activity varied, so students might register anywhere from four to eight activities per day and complete some projects in less than an hour while others continued for weeks.

Students were divided into four age groups and assigned an advisor. I advised the oldest group of twelve- to fourteen-year-olds. Every day advisors discussed with their advisees the students' plans for that and subsequent days and commented on the students' progress. Each day's plan was recorded in the students' log books. When meeting with my advisees, I attempted to ascertain how they learned best and to use this along with their skills and interests to direct their learning. For example, some students were comfortable working abstractly in mathematics while other students learned better with concrete materials like Cuisenaire rods and other manipulatives. Or I might review with a student his or her ideas about a project and explore possibilities for expansion.

Sometimes I felt it was essential to meet with all my advisees in a group. Often we discussed issues regarding learning: How do we evaluate learning and students' work? Does all work started have to be completed; if not, how do we assess what was learned? How might we build on current projects? We also met to simply share what we had been doing. Our meetings were an important part of becoming a community of learners.

I also checked when a student most recently worked in a particular subject and, if he or she had not worked in that subject recently, the reasoning. Students' rationales for their activities varied: Students may avoid subjects because they do not want to reveal their weaknesses, may not want to confront the work necessary to improve, or may be widening their interests, planning to return to neglected areas later.

Because students were given the responsibility for planning and carrying out their learning within the context of the experiences and suggestions of teachers, the students and the adult engaged in frequent negotiation. Students negotiated from their experiences, and their knowledge of their abilities, interests, and feelings. Teachers negotiated from their perception of the students and their knowledge of learning activities and resources, of how learning occurs, and of what skills are needed in this society. Furthermore, by choosing their activities, students were more likely to take ownership and responsibility for completing them.

Our new structure remedied a number of problems. Teachers could schedule times to introduce projects to students and follow through with them over days, weeks, or months. Teachers could meet with individual or groups of students without being distracted or interrupted. Teachers could get a clear sense of what their advisees were doing in different academic areas and from one day to the next. Students and teachers could negotiate what was expected from a student and why. Students could move about the school working with other students and learning from all the teachers based on their interests and needs. To understand how this worked, I offer details from an architecture and a geology unit.

LEARNING TOGETHER: RESEARCHING CITY
PLANNING FOR PUBLIC TELEVISION

While as a university student I majored in architecture for only a short time, architecture has remained an interest. Early in the second year, the elementary school moved out of the log building into a two-room schoolhouse previously housing a public school. Under the leadership of one of the new teachers, we began building lofts and other spaces in the school totally transforming the physical environment. As we moved around lofts, shelves, tables, sofas, and chairs, we talked with students about how different arrangements affected learning and teaching, and group and individual activities. The students became increasingly aware of the effects of the built environment, and began to visualize other possibilities.

Later in the school year, five students and I, while presenting at an education conference, attended a session on building school playgrounds. We returned to the school and, with the other teachers, students, and several parents, designed and built the school's playground. The students' interest in design led to a field trip to an architectural firm where the architects' drawings and models impressed the students. After that visit, I built a drafting table and students began designing buildings, drawing floor plans and elevations, and building architectural models.

In the meantime, we had been asked by the local public television affiliate to do a program on some aspect of government. While the producer proposed ideas such as "how a bill becomes a law," because of our developing interests in the built environment, we proposed a program on the Metropolitan Area Planning Association (MAPA), a regional planning agency for the Omaha metropolitan area.

We began by asking our older students if they were interested. They responded enthusiastically, in part, because of the prospect of "being on television." However, a half-hour program required more than enthusiasm. My own thinking inclined toward the political and theoretical, which not surprisingly proved too difficult for the students to research and portray. Another teacher promoted the idea of explaining MAPA by "filming a tour" of the agency with the students acting as agency employees.

Unsure of what would actually work (none of us, of course, had ever written a television program), we first tried to learn about MAPA by reading MAPA's publications, interviewing staff, and sitting in on a board meeting. Besides becoming bored, we could not figure out just what MAPA really did, in part because the agency's role in the community was evolving. None of the students could come up with feasible ideas and we began to pressure the students to develop the promised program. I realized that my ideas were inappropriate, students rejected the idea of a tour as sophomoric, and the students had few ideas of their own.

After a month or two we gave up on the project. Students and teachers were frustrated and tired. But after letting the project lay dormant for several weeks, we started to explore new ways of learning about MAPA. We toured some of their projects, met with a staff member, looked at their maps, and videotaped some "person on the street" interviews. We began to get a better understanding of issues regarding urban renewal and suburban sprawl. We set deadlines and actually began to believe that we had something to say. From that point, the students knew what they could do and completing the project was easier and more enjoyable.

In the end, we included children from ages five through fourteen in the writing and included every student in the school in some aspect of the production: writing, acting, scenery, or filming. The final program was composed of two dozen short vignettes that only children could conceive. We herded seventy students off to the studio. A few examples should convey the students' spirit.

We learned that some areas near streams and rivers were designated as "hundred-year flood plains," meaning that the area would flood, on average, once a century. Two building uses were permitted in such areas: drive-in theaters and the misleadingly named "mobile homes." Therefore, in one vignette a homeowner stands outside his front door just as it begins, through special effects, to rain. Then, as water begins to rise around the homeowner, a MAPA representative approaches to query the homeowner whether or not he knew that he lived in a flood plain, patiently showing him a regional planning map. As he does so, the mobile home floats off.

Other vignettes included can-can dancers singing a song praising city planning, and a student narrating other students' photographs portraying downtown urban renewal and the environmental effects of suburban sprawl. The program, which we titled *MAPA Who?*, was shown on public television and later used by MAPA to explain regional planning to area citizens.

Throughout the project, teachers and students frequently changed leadership roles and, at one point, everyone quit, which provided time to gain perspective and return with better ideas. The teachers were clearly in charge of the overall planning but the students owned the creative process of writing and acting. In fact, the vignettes the students wrote were more creative than we could have imagined.

Developing a television program on city planning grew out of the students' increasing interest in architecture and urban spaces and from an opportunity presented to us by the local public television station. The next part illustrates an example of when a whole unit was sparked by an interest of one student.

As already described, students had input into the day's activities. One day, as children entered the school, a five-year-old asked me if I would read to the students a book about the Grand Canyon, a book his father had brought back from a recent visit to the national park. I agreed and posted the book as one of the activities students could choose. Most of the students who signed up were five to seven years old.

Later, while sitting with students to read the book, I began by asking if they knew how the canyon was formed. The students responded by suggesting earthquakes and tornadoes as the likely causes, to which I responded that the river eroded the soil, forming the canyon. After the students exclaimed that I could not possibly be correct—they described my explanation as crazy—I offered to teach a month-long unit that would demonstrate sedimentation, erosion, and the formation of canyons. If they agreed, I would plan the unit and begin teaching in the next few days. They agreed, and for a month we explored erosion through a variety of projects. We studied the effects of rainwater on our playground and the erosion of layers of sedimentary shale and limestone in a streambed. We used a "stream table" to explore how erosion varied depending on the amount and force of water, the slope of the land, and whether the soil consisted of sand or clay. We made clay relief maps from topographical maps so that we could examine the paths water took (streams flowing into rivers and lakes) and their effects on the land.

This example demonstrates how adults can use their greater knowledge and experience to guide student learning. The curriculum grew out of the students' interest in canyons. However, they did not initially express an interest in geology; indeed, they did not know such a scientific discipline existed. Rather, as their teacher I took their nascent interest in canyons and expanded it to include the field of geology. Further, I agreed to teach the unit only when they agreed that it was something they wanted to do. After all, since geology is not typically included in the primary school curriculum, there was no harm in not teaching it and moving onto something else.

My questioning the students regarding their knowledge of geological processes depicts how I understand the difference between Holt and Dewey. Whereas Holt would wait for the students to ask, Dewey would argue that the adult has a "natural authority" based on greater experience that needs to be brought to the situation. I was not, I would argue, imposing my authority arbitrarily, but offered my greater experience and knowledge as an organizing force and resource. Dewey (1963) wrote:

> Finding the material for learning within the experience is only the first step. The next step is the progressive development of what is already experienced into a fuller and richer form, a form that gradually approximates that in which subject matter is presented to the skilled, mature person. (pp. 73–74)

RECENT PEDAGOGICAL PROJECTS

I continue to collaborate with pre-service and practicing teachers in developing units and lesson plans in which we develop interdisciplinary curriculum that build on students' knowledge and interests and use authentic assessments. For example, I am currently working with public school teachers funded by a grant from the National Institute of Environmental Health Sciences on designing and implementing units that focus on the relationship between the environment and human health.

In one suburban school, for example, fifth grade students investigated how residential use of different toxins entered a nearby stream and, therefore, polluted the watershed. In the process, students learned about historical changes in the community's land use and interpreted topographic maps, scientific tests for water purity, and alternatives to using toxins. Students concluded the unit by describing the negative environmental and health consequences from the use and misuse of pesticides and herbicides, the improper disposal of motor oil, and neglecting to clean up after your dog. The students presented this information through a variety of media, including pamphlets, posters, Power-Point presentations, videos, and websites.

Dewey wrote that schools should not merely prepare students to become democratic citizens as adults, but should be places where students already acted as democratic citizens and contributed to the community. For me this means that we should not be assessing students based primarily on how they perform on a standardized exam; instead, students and their schools should be active contributors to democratic communities, as when my students developed a television program on regional planning or created websites on reducing the negative environmental impact of pesticides, herbicides, and pet waste.

I see no reason, for example, why elementary and secondary students cannot be community historians, conducting oral histories and sifting through historical artifacts to present a timeline of how the community changed, all of which would be made available to the public through school displays and publications. Or, given that my own city of Rochester, New York, has the highest rate of childhood lead poisoning in the country, I don't see why students shouldn't become community activists providing their neighbors with information on how lead poisoning occurs and what families can do to reduce their risks. Would not reducing the number of children suffering from lead poisoning be an authentic assessment of students' learning and using science, social studies, math, arts, technology, and the language arts?

Some schools, such as those in the Performance Standards Consortium, already use a variety of assessments that focus on developing a holistic understanding of students' learning and providing students with multiple means in which they might demonstrate what they have learned. In chapter 5, I describe examples of curriculum and student projects from the Performance Standards Consortium that have been undermined if not eliminated by standardized testing requirements.

In this chapter, I gave a brief description of how we might think about teaching and learning, not with the aim of giving a definitive answer, but to suggest both the complexity of the issues we face and some possibilities of what we might do. In the remainder of this book I turn first to the ongoing debates over the purposes and organization of education and then to the more recent educational reforms—reforms that embody neoliberal theories and policies prioritizing economic growth and efficiency over understanding and equality. I fear that our recent gains in understanding both the teaching and learning process and the contribution schools can make to democratic practices and social equality will be undermined by efforts to create competitive, entrepreneurial, economic, productive individuals through high-stakes standardized testing and accountability.

4

Conflicting Visions of Schooling and Teaching: The Historical and Political Context

The current conflicts over the purpose of education, curriculum, and assessment are variations of the debates over the last century. As a beginning teacher almost four decades ago, I read John Holt's *How Children Fail* (1964), which captured both my observations regarding schools at the time and my fears for the future.

> Most children in school fail. For a great many, this failure is avowed and absolute. Close to forty percent of those who begin high school, drop out before they finish. For college, the figure is one in three.
>
> Many others fail in act if not in name. They complete their schooling only because we have agreed to push them up through the grades and out of the schools, whether they know anything or not. There are many more such children than we think. If we "raise our standards" much higher, as some would have us do, we will find out very soon just how many there are. Our classrooms will bulge with kids who can't pass the test to get into the next class.
>
> But there is a more important sense in which almost all children fail: Except for a handful, who may or may not be good students, they fail to develop more than a tiny part of the tremendous capacity for learning, understanding, and creating with which they were born and of which they made full use during the first two or three years of their lives.
>
> Why do they fail? (p. 15)

Over the last decade we have realized Holt's fears: we have "raised standards" and some states and districts require that students pass a standardized test to be promoted to the next grade or graduate from high school, resulting in an increasing number of students being retained in a grade or failing to graduate (Haney, 2000). In states like New York and Florida that require students to pass one or more standardized exams to graduate, the graduation rate hovers just over 50 percent. In many cities, less than 40 percent of the students graduate. Moreover, by focusing on test preparation, students may only memorize enough to pass the exam and then forget it. Holt's fears regarding the effects of "raising standards" have been realized.

What is most regrettable is that the ascendancy of high-stakes testing and accountability comes at a time when many of Dewey's ideas regarding the school as a community, interdisciplinary learning, and authentic assessment were not only being successfully implemented in public schools—such as the Urban Academy in New York City, the schools that make up the Performance Assessment Consortium (www.performanceassessment.org), and the schools portrayed in Mike Rose's *Possible Lives: The Promise of Public Education in America* (1995)—but also at a time when research has been validating these innovative, interdisciplinary teaching approaches. For example, the National Research Council's commissioned reports on teaching, learning, and assessment conclude that we now understand "the nature of competent performance and the principles of knowledge organization that underlie people's abilities to solve problems in a wide variety of areas," and how best to teach and assess student learning (2001, p. 4). Its report, *Knowing What Students Know: The Science and Design of Educational Assessment* (2001), specifically recommends against using a few standardized exams to assess students:

> Policy makers are urged to recognize the limitations of current assessments, and to support the development of new systems of multiple assessments that would improve their ability to make decisions about education programs and the allocation of resources. Important decisions about individuals should not be based on a single test score. Policy makers should instead invest in the development of assessment systems that use multiple measures of student performance, particularly when high stakes are attached to the results. (p. 310)

In this chapter I suggest some of the reasons why recent educational reforms focusing on high-stakes testing and accountability, which contradict what we now know about teaching and learning, have been implemented. I trace out two ongoing conflicts: the first over the purposes of schooling and the second over the nature of society.

I begin by reviewing the debates between those who argued that schools should prepare students to become productive workers and those who argued for developing democratic citizens. For the former group, historian Elizabeth Fones-Wolf (1994) writes that schools have been seen as a "means of socializing workers for the factory, and as a way of promoting social and political stability" (p. 190). As early as the nineteenth century, businesses began appealing for schools to train students to be efficient workers in the increasing global marketplace. Furthermore, schools were pressed not only to develop efficient workers, but also to increase their efficiency by adopting business models, such as, at the beginning of the 1900s, "scientific management."

For the latter group, which focuses on education for democratic citizenship, education exists to develop the social conditions and intelligence that enable citizens to make social and vocational decisions that support their own and their community's welfare. Progressive educators, like Dewey, criticized training students for the workforce as undermining "the possibility of intellectual and moral growth and, thereby, the kind of education that is, in the long run, the most durable and functional of all" (Kliebard, 1999, p. 233).

I show that throughout the last century we have witnessed the rise of what education historian Herbert Kliebard (1999) describes as vocationalism, "the idea that the curriculum as a whole, not just a part of it, exists for the purpose of getting and holding a job" (xiv). I trace the path of vocationalism from its beginnings in the late 1800s to the recent wave of reforms focusing on standards and standardized testing, which began in 1983 with the publication of *A Nation at Risk* and climaxes with the implementation of No Child Left Behind (NCLB). Furthermore, throughout the whole period, reform efforts were tied to the efforts to enable the United States to better compete economically with other countries and has evolved into what Fairclough (2006) describes as a globalist discourse, which as a nodal discourse provides a rationale for the discourses of testing and accountability. President Bush's recent statements exemplify how a globalist discourse is used to promote policies focusing on standardized testing:

> NCLB is an important way to make sure America remains competitive in the
> 21st century. We're living in a global world. See, the education system must

compete with education systems in China and India. If we fail to give our students the skills necessary to compete in the world in the 21st century, the jobs will go elsewhere. (U.S. Department of Education, 2006b, p. 2)

Such discourses dominate the popular press, as in Thomas Freidman's bestselling *The World Is Flat: A Brief History of the Twenty-first Century* (2005) and in reform proposals such as the National Center for Education and the Economy's report *Tough Choices or Tough Times* (2007). However, in chapter 7, I will argue that such globalist discourses are inaccurate, misleading, and dangerous.

The second conflict I describe examines our changing notions of freedom and the changing relationship between individuals and society and between individuals and government. During most of the twentieth century, social democratic liberalism became increasingly dominant as workers, women, and people of color pushed for and were able to extend their personal and political rights for education, housing, health, workplace safety, and the right to vote. Moreover, after World War II, workers, through organizing and strikes, were able to increase their wages. From the 1940s to the early 1970s, median incomes rose and the income gap between whites and people of color and between women and men decreased (Hacker, 1993). From the 1950s through the 1970s, schools became less segregated, Title I funding for urban students increased, and the achievement gap between white students and students of color decreased (Berliner & Biddle, 1995).

However, social democratic liberalism was always contested and neoliberals, who seek to privatize social services and reduce the role of government to regulating markets, have become increasingly vocal and influential. Because *neoliberalism* is not a term familiar to most educators, I show how neoliberalism differs from *social democratic liberalism* (which is what most people think of as liberalism) and how it is similar to but different from *classical liberalism*. Consequently, the most recent education reforms have not only promoted standardized testing and accountability, but also have called for converting public education into a market system with parental and student choice, and privatizing education as much as possible. In the remainder of this chapter and book I show how neoliberal theory informs much of the recent reform efforts and what vision of school and society we might offer in its place.

THE RISE OF VOCATIONALISM

Kliebard, in *Schooled to Work: Vocationalism and the American Curriculum: 1876–1946* (1999), documents how vocational education and vocationalization were used to solve political and economic problems, including economic recessions and depressions, the perceived inadequacies of immigrants, and increased global economic competition. Both Kliebard (1999) and Wirth (1972) begin their analysis of the rise of "scientific management" and vocational education by examining the economic recession of the 1893, when industrial representatives, in particular the newly formed National Association of Manufacturers (NAM), attributed the recession to superior European vocational education systems. In response, the NAM sent representatives to study the German schools and returned convinced that American corporations could successfully compete only if the American school system became a "training ground for the workplace" by developing separate vocational schools using the German model as a prototype (Wirth, 1977, p. 163). Kliebard describes how the NAM used the economic recession to call for increased educational efficiency by modeling schools after factories. In their desire to "make the United States preeminent in the international marketplace," they were, writes Kliebard (1999), particularly concerned with

> the excellence of Germany's manufactured goods, an advantage manufacturers attributed to the German system of vocational education. . . . Just as the modern factory required exacting blueprints for the products to be produced and predetermined production goals in order to be truly efficient, so now did the schools require exacting determination of the outcomes to be achieved in relation to the raw material. (pp. 27–28)

At almost the same time that the NAM was calling for increasing educational efficiency, Frederick Winslow Taylor, "the father of scientific management," delivered his first paper (1895) on how to increase worker productivity. Taylor promoted time-motion studies of the workplace so that all workers could be instructed and coerced into using "the one right way" of carrying out their tasks. "Under Taylor's system of scientific management," writes Kliebard (1999), "foremen would be replaced by efficiency experts, an exacting standardization of work, and the stopwatch as a mechanism of controls. Workers would then be expected to submit to the strict regulation that Taylor imposed in return for higher wages" (p. 46).

Scientific management and the centrality of schools as places in which students were prepared for the world of work became the principal response to the massive increase in immigration to the United States from eastern and southern European countries in the early 1900s. Among the questions educators and society faced were: Could schools accommodate more students and, if so, how? Should we have the same expectations of all students and, therefore, deliver the same education to all, or have different expectations and, therefore, different curricula? Scientific management provided an answer.

The influence of Taylor's ideas grew so that, by the time he published *The Principles of Scientific Management* in 1911, he was considered a "cultural hero" (Kliebard, 1999, p. 47) whose ideas were of interest to all, not least educators, including John Franklin Bobbitt, Robert Yerkes, and David Snedden. Bobbitt wrote the first books on curriculum, titled simply *The Curriculum* (1918) and *How to Make a Curriculum* (1924). Yerkes promoted mental measurement via standardized testing so that we could sort students into tracks for their "probable destinies." And Snedden, who assumed the powerful post of commissioner of education for the Commonwealth of Massachusetts, applied the principles of scientific management to the organization of schools and pedagogy. Whereas schools are sometimes compared metaphorically to factories, these three people literally conceptualized schools *as* factories.

Bobbitt, in his 1912 article, "The Elimination of Waste in Education," extolled the virtues of a school in Gary, Indiana, that adopted the factory model, called itself "a school plant," and was led by an "educational engineer." Bobbitt commended the Gary school system for its efficient use of space and time—students moved around the building in a platoon system so that every room was in constant use—and for "operating the plant" from morning until evening, including weekends. Furthermore, the school provided students with different curricula based on their different abilities. Bobbitt (1912) equated educating students to manufacturing products:

> work up that raw material into the finished product for which it is best adapted. Applied to education this means: Educate the individual according to his capabilities. This requires that the materials of the curriculum be sufficiently various to meet the needs of every class of individuals in the community; and that the

course of training and study be sufficiently flexible that the individual can be given just the things he needs. (p. 269)

Bobbitt, observes Kliebard (1999),

set forth a principle that became central to the process of schooling in the twentieth century: "Education is primarily for adult life, not for child life. Its fundamental responsibility is to prepare for the fifty years of adulthood, not of the twenty years of childhood and youth" (Bobbitt, 1924, p. 8). (p. 53)

If we are to "educate individuals according to their capabilities," then we need, argued Yerkes and Snedden, to determine individuals' capabilities. At the same time that Bobbitt proposed adjusting curriculum according to students' capabilities, hereditarians developed the first tests to assess individuals' intelligence. Robert Yerkes, an early promoter of intelligence tests, developed and administered intelligence tests to World War I army recruits, which was the first case of mass administered IQ testing (Gould, 1981, p. 194). Stephen Jay Gould, in *The Mismeasure of Man* (1981), exposed the tests for the charade they were: culturally biased, with directions that were incomprehensible to test takers because they either did not understand English or did not understand the purpose and concept of standardized testing. Gould concluded "that the conditions of testing, and the basic character of the examination, made it ludicrous to believe that [the tests] measured any internal state deserving the label intelligence" (p. 210).

Whatever their faults, Yerkes (1919) argued that the army mental measurements "demonstrated most convincingly the practicality of methods of mental testing for the classification and placement of men," which now could be applied to "examining school children by groups" (p. 6) so that they could be placed in the appropriate education tracks according to their predetermined destinies. He proposed that when children arrived at school, they would be placed into one of three groups with the highest scoring group educated to become "professionals," the middle group prepared for "industrial" careers, and the lowest scoring group trained to become "manual workers." Thus, educational tracking was born.

Finally, David Snedden declared that the "fundamental idea in education . . . is to make men efficient" (cited in Drost, 1967, pp. 67–68). Snedden, in

"Education for a World of Team-Players and Team Workers" (1924), compared society to a crew on a submarine, with a commander, a few officers, and numerous subordinates, and asserted that schools should prepare a few students to be leaders, while training the vast majority "to follow." Fortunately, stated Snedden, deciding which students should be selected as leaders only required knowing students' "probable destinies," which coincided with existing inequalities in students' gender, race, and class. A few white males would be tracked into leadership positions; the rest were consigned to subordinate roles. Schools, for Snedden, should be assessed on how much they contribute to economic growth and not on whether they promote economic equality or critical citizenship.

The promotion of education for work leads Kliebard (1999) to conclude that vocationalism has become the dominant way in which we conceptualize education. He states:

> By borrowing the language of the workplace, vocationalism applies the conceptual apparatus associated with business and industry to the enterprise of schooling. The content of school subjects is not simply oriented to the workplace; schooling is actually conceived and understood in terms of raw material and finished products, gains and loses, inputs and outputs, productive and unproductive labor, elimination of waste, return on investment, precise production goals, and of course, the bottom line. . . . To the extent that vocationalism becomes the controlling purpose of schooling, our senses of what constitutes pedagogical success and failure is governed by its strictures. (p. 121)

However, social efficiency was not uncontested. John Dewey was one of many progressives who opposed social efficiency proponents such as Bobbitt and Snedden, arguing that the primary purpose of education was developing critical democratic citizens. For Dewey, all social institutions, including workplaces, should facilitate personal growth and be judged on the "contribution they make to the all-around growth of every member of society" (Dewey, 1950, p. 147). Dewey and Snedden publicly debated one another in the *New Republic,* where Dewey (1915) disagreed with the idea that students were to be prepared for the needs of business and stated that he was not interested in adapting students to the "existing industrial regime," but, instead, wanted them to "transform it" (p. 42). Dewey wanted schools to create citizens who would push workplaces to become democratic and institutions should be assessed based on their contribution to human development rather than "a senseless pursuit of profits" (Wirth, 1977, p. 169).

For Dewey (1987), schools were essential to developing the "democratic habits of thought and action" necessary for effective participation in the democratic process (p. 225). As I described in earlier chapters, Dewey conceptualized freedom not as the right to do what one pleases (see Dewey's *Experience and Education*, 1963) but, rather, as existing in relationship with others so that people, as a community, engage in the task of improving themselves and society. Achieving this goal requires that individuals deliberate with one another and practice habits of "open-mindedness, tolerance of diversity, fairness, rational understanding, respect for truth, and critical judgment" (Olssen, Codd & O'Neill, 2004, p. 269). Dewey believed schooling was essential for developing deliberative democracy.

Dewey was not alone in his criticism and the capitalist crisis of the Great Depression of 1930 invigorated the education debate. George Counts, in his 1932 speech, "Dare the School Build a New Social Order?" explicitly challenged teachers to develop a democratic, socialist society. His call came at a time when many were questioning whether capitalism was tenable. In the journal *The Social Frontier* (1934–1939), social reconstructionists such as Dewey, Counts, Charles Beard, and Harold Rugg called for reforming the economic system to serve the public's rather than corporate needs. Teachers, argued Counts (1932), if they used a curriculum that promoted a critical study of contemporary economic, social, and political problems, could "remake the world" (pp. 261–262). Rugg (1923) believed that society required a thorough social reconstruction and that could best be accomplished through education. To this end, Rugg, seeing the curriculum as central to what could be accomplished, developed a series of social studies textbooks that rather than presenting the United States as a flawless democratic beacon for the world, focused on social issues and problems.

Not surprisingly, the ideas and activities of the social reconstructionists were vigorously opposed by conservative educators and corporate leaders who denounced using education to examine the dominant vocationalist approach to education. During the depression, the United States Chamber of Commerce led a campaign to reduce school taxes and slash school budgets. Leaders of the "National Association of Manufacturers and the Chamber of Commerce joined the [American] Legion in charging that collectivists [a term used for those who wanted a less individualistic approach] were indoctrinating students through [Rugg's textbooks] and reducing the younger generation's trust in the free enterprise system" (Fones-Wolfe, 1994, pp. 190–191). Organizations, supported by the Daughters of the Colonial Wars and Bertie Forbes of *Forbes* magazine, successfully forced the removal of Ruggs' texts from the schools.

After the depression, the National Association of Manufacturers teamed with the National Education Association (then primarily an organization of school administrators, now an organization for teachers) to promote corporate interests in schools. For example, at a jointly sponsored 1945 conference, the schools were urged to "indoctrinate the students with the American way of life" and teach that "the American system of free enterprise has done more for human comforts than any other system" (Fones-Wolfe, 1994, p. 200), thus revealing that they were not against indoctrination, as long as corporations and those in power did the indoctrinating. Their efforts aimed to rid the schools of any criticisms of the U.S. economic system and to prepare students through teaching and tracking for their "appropriate" place in the workforce. As World War II came to a close, business leaders mounted a campaign urging women to leave paid work and to return home, thus ending the career of "Rosie the Riveter."

When the U.S emerged from World War II as a world leader relatively unscathed by the war, reformers increasingly tied education and worker productivity not only to corporate efficiency but also to economic and military competition with other countries. When the Soviet Union launched *Sputnik* in 1957, political leaders feared that the United States was falling behind the Soviet Union both militarily and educationally, particularly in math and science. *Sputnik* spurred the federal government to pass the National Defense Education Act (1958), which began:

> The Congress hereby finds and declares that the security of the nation requires the fullest development of the mental resources and technical skills of its young men and women. . . . The defense of this Nation depends upon the mastery of modern techniques developed from complex scientific principles. (cited in Kliebard, 1986, p. 266)

The act focused on curriculum reform in math, science, and foreign languages. As Kliebard notes, most of the funding was funneled through the National Science Foundation, established in 1950 as part of the executive branch of government, and funding primarily went to university researchers. The National Defense Education Act marked the beginning of federal efforts to influence the curriculum, a development that has become more pronounced over time.

The mid-1950s also brought the beginning of the civil rights movement, with most notably, the 1954 Supreme Court decision *Brown v. Board of Education* outlawing school segregation as separate and unequal, and the 1955 Montgomery bus boycott, precipitated by Rosa Parks, ending segregation on public transportation. While the 1950s are often described as quiescent, they in fact marked the beginning of not only the civil rights but also other movements for economic and social equality, including gender and welfare rights. Moreover, even with restrictive laws, such as the Taft-Hartley Act, workers gained strength and increasingly fought for and achieved better working conditions.

While desegregation was fiercely resisted in many cities, some schools, school districts, and residential areas were integrated. Integration contributed to increasing educational achievement by Hispanic and black students from the 1960s until the 1990s. For example, the National Assessment of Education Progress (NAEP), conducted by the National Center for Educational Statistics and the best, if still flawed, assessment of student learning in the United States, shows that from the 1970s into the 1990s, black and Hispanic students substantially reduced the achievement gap with white students (Berliner & Biddle, 1995). While over the last two decades many on the political right have criticized the educational practices that existed previous to the recent accountability reforms, the data show that the achievement gap was closing under the "old" postwar reforms. However, as I will demonstrate later, it is under the current reforms, which ostensibly aim to close the gap, to "leave no child behind," that the gap has remained the same or widened.

What became the opening round in the current fight over high-stakes testing and accountability occurred in 1983, when the Reagan administration sponsored the report, *A Nation at Risk,* which was highly critical of American public education. During the early 1980s, as in the 1890s, Americans experienced a recession, intentionally induced by the Reagan administration as a means of reducing workers' demands for higher wages (Henwood, 2003, pp. 208–209). However, blame of the high unemployment rate and falling wages was diverted away from the policies of the Reagan administration and the

Federal Reserve Bank and onto the education system, a process of "exporting the blame" described in detailed by Michael Apple (1996). *A Nation at Risk* claimed, without providing evidence, that the "average achievement of high school students on most standardized tests is now lower than 26 years ago when Sputnik was launched" (NCEE, p. 8) and such a "rising tide of mediocrity" was eroding "the educational foundations of our society" that threatened "our very future as a Nation and a people" (p. 5).

Since *A Nation at Risk*, schooling in the United States has undergone numerous reform waves, most led not by educators but by corporate executives and governmental representatives. Initial reforms focused on developing and implementing standards, but these soon transformed into efforts to hold schools, teachers, and students accountable through high-stakes testing. Some states, such as Texas, Florida, and New York, imposed requirements that students pass several standardized tests in order to graduate from high school. However, it was the No Child Left Behind Act, passed in 2001, in which the federal government imposed high-stakes testing on students throughout the country.

While students face increased testing, schools are becoming re-segregated. The advances in integration and academic achievement for students of color from the late 1950s through 1980s began to unravel in the 1990s. As mentioned, numerous Supreme Court decisions, including the most recent decision involving the desegregation plans for Louisville and Seattle (*Community Schools v. Seattle School District #1*, June 28, 2007) outlawed almost all the methods through which urban schools could desegregate (Orfield & Eaton, 1996). Many urban school districts are currently composed of 80 to 90 percent black and Hispanic students with some schools having less than 1 percent white students (Kozol, 2005, pp. 8–9). Consequently, while the achievement gap between white students and students of color narrowed following *Brown v. Board of Education*, with re-segregation and the introduction of testing and accountability measures, the gap has widened. "There was a tremendous amount of gap narrowing in the '70s and '80s but 'somewhere around 1990, the gap-narrowing stopped,'" according to Craig Jerald of the Education Trust (cited in Kozol, 2005, p. 381).

Schools, after progress following *Brown v. Board of Education*, are becoming increasingly segregated and unequal. Furthermore, first states and then the federal government have imposed high-stakes standardized testing and accountability, along with threats of privatization for failing to achieve required test score increases, on local schools and districts. Over the last several decades, educators have had less say over what and how they teach, as many schools, particularly those in which students are more likely to have difficulty passing standardized tests, focus on preparing for those tests.

To understand this shift requires not only that we understand that schools have often been used to satisfy corporate desires for more productive employees, but also the shift in which society is conceptualized; from social democratic liberalism to neoliberalism. Understanding the shift from social democratic liberalism to neoliberalism helps us to understand the political and economic assumptions underlying the current efforts toward school choice, competition, testing, and accountability.

THE RISE OF NEOLIBERALISM AND
THE DECLINE OF THE WELFARE STATE

Neoliberal theory and practices have become so embedded within our economic and political decision making that neoliberalism is rarely explicitly invoked as a rationale. Yet, the education reform movement of the last several decades could neither be conceptualized nor instituted without the rise and supremacy of neoliberal thought. Therefore, understanding and resisting the recent reforms requires comprehending the neoliberal principles that guide policies.

Moreover, not only is neoliberalism rarely discussed, but also, because neoliberalism has been most strongly identified with the current Bush administration and the past administrations of Reagan and Thatcher, some find the term *neoliberalism* confusing. Some assume that a "neo" or "new" form of liberalism should connect to and build on the past social democratic liberal policies of Franklin Roosevelt, John Kennedy, or Lyndon Johnson. To understand how neoliberalism relates to both current Republican and past Democratic administrations requires understanding the transformations liberalism has undergone from the late sixteenth century to the present.

Therefore, after giving a short definition of neoliberalism, I provide a brief overview of the history of liberalism, including the similarities and differences between previous forms of liberalism and neoliberalism. Then, I will describe some of the ways in which neoliberalism influences current social and education policies. Lastly, while neoliberalism is often assumed to be the last and enduring stage of capitalism, neoliberalism's contradictions and failings may result in either significant modifications or the demise of neoliberalism.

David Harvey, in *A Brief History of Neoliberalism* (2005), defines neoliberalism as "a theory of political economic practices that proposes that human well-being can best be advanced by liberating individual entrepreneurial freedoms and skills within an institutional framework characterized by strong private property rights, free markets and free trade." Such practices require that "the state create and preserve an institutional framework appropriate to such practices," (p. 2) including international organizations, such as the World Bank and International Monetary Fund, that pressure national governments to eliminate trade barriers and reduce social spending. Neoliberal policies also call for privatizing education through charter school and voucher programs and converting education into a competitive market system, all of which are evident in recent policies at the local, state, and federal levels.

Neoliberalism is most similar to the original or classical version of liberalism, which began in the seventeenth century and, in one form or another, has been the dominant philosophical, political, and economic theory since. Liberalism first emerged as the philosophical and political rationale for opposing the authority of the church and monarchy. In place of obedience to the church and crown, liberal social philosophers, including Locke (1960/1690), Hobbes (1968/1651), and Voltaire (2000/1763) put forward the "principles of civil rights, rights of property, a limited conception of state power and a broadly negative conception of freedom" (Olssen, Codd & O'Neill, 2004, p. 80). Liberalism reconceptualized the relationship between the individual and the secular and sacred state, aiming to free individuals from state interference and portraying individuals as pursuing their self-interest, which, coincidently, also served societal interests and promoted social progress.

Such political views soon influenced economic theories, and the idea that society could best be served by individuals pursuing their self-interest was reflected in Adam Smith's (*Wealth of Nations*, 1776) notion of the "invisible hand." Smith argued that individuals, in pursuing their own interests, brought benefits to everyone and that this could best be accomplished in a market system that "brought economic gains to each party, and ultimately to the nation as a whole" (Olssen, Codd & O'Neill, 2004, p. 88).

Liberalism revolutionized Western European society. The ways in which people conceptualized and talked about individuals and society and the kinds of social practices that could be carried out were transformed. Representative governments and the rule of law replaced the monarchy. Societies industrialized and their overall wealth grew.

But industrialization and wealth came at a cost—increased wealth for a few and increased poverty for many. One need only think of the society described by Victorian writers such as Charles Dickens. Consequently, workers began to organize and demand better working conditions and the general public called for laws to protect women and children from excessive labor and their families from poverty. Cities and states passed legislation in relation to education, employment, health, and other issues with the increasing acknowledgment that local and state governments must be involved in social and economic affairs by providing the conditions for all people to realize their capacities.

The Great Depression further exposed the shortcomings of classical liberalism. In the United States, Roosevelt responded by implementing Keynesian economic theories, in which the state used spending, tax, and welfare policies to rebuild the country and to fund the military effort in World War II. The United States emerged from the war victorious and Keynesian economics and social democratic liberalism were to remain dominant up to the 1970s.

The decades immediately after the war were marked by "the historic compromise" between capital and labor in which, in exchange for improving wages, labor consented to capital's right not only to control the workplace but also to allow capitalist control of investment and growth, primarily through the growth of multinational corporations. At the same time workers, women, and people of color struggled for and were able to extend their personal and political rights for education, housing, health, workplace safety, and the right to vote (Bowles & Gintis, 1986, pp. 57–59). Legal school segregation was ended by the courts, if not ended in practice. States expanded and opened up their systems of higher education to more students. With the growth of the welfare state, the number of governmental jobs increased and, with racial discrimination more difficult, more African Americans and people of color gained decent paying positions. From the end of World War II until the early 1970s, the income gap between whites and people of color and between men and women decreased at a significant rate (Hacker, 1993). And, fueled in part by workers' growing wages, the immediate postwar period was marked by unusually rapid and stable economic growth.

However, efforts to expand personal and political rights were not uncontested. For persons of color, the right to vote was won only through unrelenting, heroic, and sometimes lethal struggle and is still, given the recent electoral irregularities in Florida and Ohio, precarious. Similarly, in the United States, Social Security benefits were denied to many African Americans when Congress surrendered to Southern politicians' demands to exclude agricultural and domestic household workers, jobs typically filled by African Americans (Katznelson, 2005). Even the now-venerated G.I. Bill for returning veterans "roused the ire of all but the most moderate business leaders . . . [who] disliked the liberal agenda and felt that the New Deal traditions associated with the Labor movement and the Democratic Party continued to appeal to American workers" (Fones-Wolfe, 1994, p. 7).

During the era in which social democratic liberalism dominated, neoliberal theorists increased their criticism, condemning social democratic liberalism as "collectivist, socialist, and economically misguided" (Levitas, 1986, p. 3). Leading U.S. neoliberals, such as Milton Friedman (1952, 1962), Robert Nozick (1974), James Buchanan (1975), and Gary Becker (1976), shared a commitment to individual liberty and limiting the state's role to enabling markets to function. Such attacks increased during the late 1960s, as businesses' net rate of profit began to fall (Parenti, 1999, p. 118). Because falling profits were attributed primarily to the inability of businesses to pass increasing wage costs on to consumers in the increasingly competitive and open world economy, part of the solution for emerging neoliberals was to squeeze workers' wages. Paul Volcker, the chairman of the Federal Reserve Bank under President Carter and later President Reagan, stated, "the average wage of workers has to decline" (cited in Bowles & Gintis, p. 60). Volcker raised interest rates, thus beginning "a long recession that would empty factories and break unions in the United States and drive debtor countries to the brink of insolvency, beginning the long era of structural adjustment" (Henwood, 2003, p. 208).

As the "Volcker shock" was being implemented in the United States, Margaret Thatcher in England attacked unions, dismantled or rolled back commitments to the welfare state, privatized public enterprises such as housing and the railroads, reduced taxes, encouraged entrepreneurial initiatives, and worked to create a favorable business climate. Ronald Reagan reduced public spending, attacked and dismantled unions (such as the air traffic controllers union PATCO), and deregulated numerous industries including airlines and communication (Harvey, 2005, pp. 23–27). Together, Thatcher, Reagan, and their corporate supporters aimed to restore higher rates of profit through neoliberal policies emphasizing "the deregulation of the economy, trade liberalization, the dismantling of the public sector [such as education, health, and social welfare], and the predominance of the financial sector of the economy over production and commerce" (Vilas, 1996, p. 16). Tabb (2002) wrote:

> [Neoliberal policies stress] the privatization of the public provision of goods and services—moving their provision from the public sector to the private—along with deregulating how private producers can behave, giving greater scope to the single-minded pursuit of profit and showing significantly less regard for the need to limit social costs or for redistribution based on nonmarket criteria. The aim of neoliberalism is to put into question all collective structures capable of obstructing the logic of the pure market. (p. 7)

But neoliberalism not only transforms the purpose of society from providing for the welfare of individuals to supporting the pursuit of profit: neoliberalism changes the relations between the individual and society. Neoliberalism expands on classic liberalism's faith in individual's pursuing their self-interest within markets by reconceptualizing the individual as not merely making choices but as an autonomous entrepreneur responsible for his or her own self, progress, and position; responsible for their own success and failure.

Mark Olssen, John Codd, and Ann-Marie McNeil (2004) write that under neoliberalism:

> Every social transaction is conceptualized as entrepreneurial, to be carried out purely for personal gain. The market introduces competition as the structuring mechanism through which resources and status are allocated efficiently and fairly. The "invisible hand" of the market is thought to be the most efficient way of sorting out which competing individuals get what. (p. 137–138)

Neoliberalism returns to classic liberalism with a vengeance. Individuals are transformed into "entrepreneurs of themselves" (Foucault, 1979), operating within a marketplace that now includes services such as education, health care, and pensions. The transformation is perhaps best characterized by a recent financial services advertisement that suggests we think of families as corporations, whose rising or falling "value" can be assessed each day just as the stock market lists corporations' values.

However, as I will further describe in chapter 7, neoliberalism has not been uncontested. In numerous countries that have adopted strong neoliberal policies, New Zealand, Chile, Argentina (to name a few), citizens have been able to repeal some of the neoliberal policies, and globally groups have organized against the World Bank's and World Trade Organization's policies.

NEOLIBERALISM AND EDUCATION

For neoliberals, markets, individual choice, and privatization are democratic and efficient solutions. Over the last twenty years, neoliberal ideals have increasingly dominated education policy. Whitty, Power, and Halpin (1998), Robertson (2000), and others (Hatcher, 2003) have described how the United States, England, and other countries embraced markets and choice as a means of improving education. Whitty, Power, and Halpin (1998) analyzed the changing educational system in five countries and conclude, "within the range of political rationales, it is the neo-liberal alternative which dominates, as does a particular emphasis on market mechanisms" (p. 35). They describe how proponents of market reforms argue that they will lead to more efficient and effective schools. Similarly, Robertson (2000) notes, "Much of the choice/markets agenda has been shaped by the criticism of schools as inefficient bureaucracies that are unresponsive either to community or individual interests." Schools, and particularly teachers, are unresponsive, write the critics, because they know parents cannot take their children elsewhere. Therefore, proponents of choice and markets argue, "efficiency and equity in education could only be addressed through 'choice' and where family or individuals were constructed as the customers of educational services" (p. 174). Increasing the range of parents' choices over their children's schools and funding schools based on the number of students that they attract introduces a competitive market approach to the allocation of resources.

Martin Thrupp and Robert Willmott (2003) note that by "the mid-1990s, Gewirtz and colleagues wrote that the 'market solution (to just about everything) currently holds politicians around the world in its thrall. . . . Schools in England are now set within the whole paraphernalia of a market system'" (p. 13). Market promoters decry "state intervention because it is held that administrative and bureaucratic structures are inherently inferior to markets as a means of allocating resources." Instead, resources are allocated through "spontaneous exchanges between individuals" (p. 18). Markets, they assume, permit individuals to make choices based on the available data and to choose well. However, as Thrupp and Willmott (2003) point out, all markets, ranging from international trade to local farmers' markets and school choice, depend on the state for regulation (Sayer, 1995, p. 87). In education, such regulation exists in the form of the standardized testing, reporting (whether as "school report cards" in New York or "league tables" in England), and bureaucratic structures in which preferences are recorded and selections made.

Furthermore, the shift toward promoting corporate over social welfare redefines the relationship between the individual and society. Under previous social democratic liberal policies, social justice required decreasing inequality through social programs and a redistribution of resources and power (Levitas, 1998, p. 14). Under neoliberal policies, inequality is a result of individuals' inadequacy, which is to be remedied not by "increasing dependency" through social welfare, but by requiring that individuals strive to become productive members of the workforce. Neoliberal governments take less responsibility for the welfare of the individual; the individual becomes responsible for him or herself. The goal for neoliberal societies is to create the competitive, instrumentally rational individual who can compete in the marketplace (Peters, 1994).

Because employability and economic productivity become central, education becomes less concerned with developing the well-rounded liberally educated person and more concerned with developing the skills required to become an economically productive member of society. Robertson (2000) describes the changing mandate as requiring that "educational systems, through creating appropriately skilled and entrepreneurial citizens and workers able to generate new and added economic values, will enable nations to be responsive to changing conditions within the international marketplace" (p. 187).

Neoliberal governments, therefore, desire to reduce funding for education while at the same time reorganizing education to fit the needs of the economy. Because the public might object to cuts in social spending and increasing economic inequality, neoliberal policymakers have skillfully packaged the reforms to make it appear that they are promoting equality. As I will describe, they use discourses emphasizing increasing education fairness, such as "requiring all students to achieve high standards as measured by objective tests," and opportunity, such as "leaving no child behind."

Another way in which neoliberal governments are able to retain their legitimacy is by blaming schools for the essential injustices and contradictions of capitalism, while they preserve inequalities through other policies, such as taxation and social spending reductions (Dale, 1989). As stated earlier, the authors of *A Nation at Risk* (1982) connected education to the economy by explicitly blaming schools for the Reagan-induced economic recession of the early 1980s (Parenti, 1999) and for the United States falling behind other countries economically. These reports shift the blame for increasing economic inequality away from the decisions made by corporations and politicians and onto the educational system. Moreover, because they frame schools as the root of our economic problems, by proposing education reforms they appear to be doing something. As Michael Apple (1996) describes, "governments must be seen to be doing something. . . . Reforming education is not only widely acceptable and relatively unthreatening, but just as crucially, its success or failure will not be obvious in the short term" (p. 88).

Focusing on educational reform not only diverts attention away from the negative implications of other policies, but also transforms the way in which we understand the relationship between the individual and society. The individual becomes central; society and the community become less important. Consequently, by shifting responsibility for individual welfare away from society as a whole to the individual, fewer expect society to provide an adequate education.

This individualism is also reflected in the way in which education is organized. In the past, when students attended schools in their own community, they and their parents had a common stake with other parents over the quality of the school, including voting for school board candidates and the amount of local school tax. Schools have had a long history of local control, with families committed to making schools work because the school was the community school. Children would attend the same schools their parents had and their siblings do and families would become involved in the welfare of the school. Parents were more likely to know other parents in their neighborhood and discuss curriculum and pedagogical concerns.

However, under school choice, as promoted in the United States by vouchers, charter schools, and No Child Left Behind (2001), parents are encouraged to transfer their children from school to school, therefore undermining their allegiance to the local school and their incentive to engage in public discourse regarding the nature and purpose of schooling. Because, as I will describe, the reforms focus on turning schools into competitive markets in which students apply to the school they want to attend, children and their parents no longer have shared interests with other students and families and, instead, become competitors for the available openings.

Lastly, not only have governments blamed schools for economic inequality, they propose that systems of standards, testing, and choice will increase educational efficiency and improve education for all. But, because neoliberal doctrine aims to reduce the size of the state and conservative doctrine claims to desire to intervene less in individual's private lives, governments have been careful not to directly intervene in the everyday practices of schools. Consequently, the state has devised a system in which they can govern schools from afar through policies promoting testing, accountability, and choice—what Stephen Ball (1994) describes as "steering from a distance" (p. 54). Such policies, rather than educating students to be critical democratic citizens, are more likely to drive all but the wealthiest schools to focus on teaching the basic skills rather than complex, interdisciplinary learning.

In the next chapter, therefore, I describe how standardized testing and accountability have been implemented at the state level, focusing on New York and Texas, and at the federal level through NCLB, and analyze the consequences of the reforms for student learning, teaching, and educational equality.

5

The Rise of High-Stakes Testing at the State and Federal Levels: New York, Texas, and No Child Left Behind

Until recently, decisions regarding curriculum and assessment were made at the classroom, school, and district levels. However, beginning in the 1980s, states began to develop subject-area standards and some states, such as Texas, New York, and Florida, began to require that students pass several standardized exams to graduate from high school, therefore making the tests high-stakes for students and their teachers. Now, the No Child Left Behind (NCLB) Act mandates that states develop standards and standardized tests in reading, math, and science, and administer the tests in grades three through eight plus once in high school. Consequently, in states such as New York, the combined federal and state testing requirements result in students facing a minimum of thirty-three standardized exams during their school career. Moreover, even though states may have no explicit state curricula, the standardized testing requirements result in a de facto state curriculum as teachers feel pressured to prepare students for the tests by focusing on what they think will be tested. Lastly, the rise of testing and other requirements at the state and federal levels have shifted control over educational decisions away from students, their families, classroom teachers, school-based and district administrators, and school board members, toward education officials and legislators at the state and federal levels.

I begin this chapter by reviewing the rise of high-stakes standardized testing in New York, the state in which I have most experience, and Texas, which served as the model for George Bush and his first secretary of education, Rod Paige, as examples of the reforms in particular states, and then turn to NCLB itself, which was signed into law in January 2002. In describing the policy changes in New York, I begin by reviewing the state of secondary education previous to the rise of high-stakes standardized testing, which included both traditional high schools dividing students into two tracks, those students presumed bound for university and those not, and nontraditional high schools— schools that later were to compose the Performance Standards Consortium (hereafter the Consortium Schools)—such as Central Park East (see Deborah Meier's *The Power of Their Ideas: Lessons for America from a Small School in Harlem*, 1995), in which students were not tracked, but taught using an interdisciplinary curriculum and assessed through portfolios and projects.

In describing the rise of high-stakes testing at the state and federal levels, I also cite the rationales presented by their proponents. In New York, for example, one of the rationales for requiring all students to pass five standardized exams to graduate was to eliminate the unequal system of tracking that permitted some students to slide through and graduate from high school without a rigorous education. Further, proponents of high-stakes testing have argued that standardized tests are more objective and rigorous than portfolios and other forms of teacher-developed assessment. However, whether high-stakes testing has resulted in an improved education for some or most is (based on the effects testing has had on schools, students, and the curriculum) questionable. Therefore, after summarizing some of the central rationales for the reforms, I provide evidence that in New York the tests have neither been as rigorous nor objective as proponents claim, have not eliminated the tracking of students, and have made it more difficult for innovative schools like the Consortium Schools to provide the challenging education that they have in the past.

Proponents for NCLB used the high-stakes testing reforms in New York and Texas to argue for instituting standardized testing nationally. I show, therefore, that many of the same reform rationales used in New York were repeated in promoting NCLB, which not only requires standardized testing but imposes consequences for schools and districts that fail to achieve "adequate yearly progress." However, NCLB exceeds statewide reforms in its curriculum requirements (for example, *Reading First*) and in the consequences schools face for failing to exceed the minimum test-score threshold, including privatization of the school's administration or the school itself and the conversion of schools into competitive markets. Bush has also attempted to include vouchers in both the initial setup of and reauthorization of NCLB.

NEW YORK: THE RISE OF STANDARDIZED TESTS AS A GRADUATION REQUIREMENT

In New York, the state's commissioner of education and the New York State Regents, who are appointed by the state assembly, govern all the state's education institutions, whether private or public, and from birth through adulthood. The chancellor is appointed as chair of the Regents.

For most of the last century, the Regents has permitted secondary schools to award students either the Regents diploma, achieved by passing a set minimum number of Regents subject area exams and courses, or a local diploma, determined by local school districts' governing boards. Consequently, during that time, New York public schools, like most schools in the United States, offered different curricula for different students and track or stream students depending on their "probable futures." Typically, university-bound students enrolled in the ostensibly more difficult Regents courses, and students not planning on attending university enrolled in the easier local courses. During the most recent decades, in New York urban districts, only approximately 30 to 70 percent of students graduated and a majority of them received local diplomas.

However, some urban schools, almost all in New York City, opted out of the two-track system and preferred developing innovative, rigorous non-Regents program for all students. These schools often developed an innovative integrated curriculum, in which students were not assessed through standardized exams but by exhibits, portfolios, and performances. In the 1990s, twenty-eight of the schools formed the Performance Standards Consortium. I have served on the board that oversees the schools, and I have often visited and am familiar with two of the schools. As I will describe, beginning in the late 1990s, the New York State Education Department explicitly required that the Consortium Schools eliminate their innovative curriculum and, instead, require that their students pass the five Regents exams in order to graduate. Examining this conflict reveals how little the state values innovative, challenging, interdisciplinary curriculum, particularly for its urban students.

The most well known of the Consortium Schools is Central Park East in New York City, founded in 1974 as a primary school, later becoming a secondary school with its first graduating class in 1991. Its founder, past principal, and most well-known advocate has been Deborah Meier, author of *The Power of Their Ideas: Lessons for America from a Small School in Harlem* (1995), which describes many of the underlying principles of not only Central Park East, but the other Consortium Schools.

Central Park East and the other Consortium Schools have been, by any measure, inordinately successful. While the characteristics of their student population have been roughly equivalent to other schools in New York City, the percentage of students graduating from high school and later university has been much higher. About 90 percent of ninth-grade students attending Consortium Schools graduate four years later and about 90 percent of those continue on to university. In comparison, approximately 35 percent of New York City ninth-grade students graduate from high school.

While each of the Consortium Schools is unique, they share certain characteristics. They are all small compared to the typical urban secondary school. Most have a few hundred students, while many secondary schools in the United States have several thousand students. And unlike the typical school, which often focuses on "covering" the material likely to be tested, therefore sacrificing depth and complexity for breadth, the Consortium Schools focus on in-depth interdisciplinary thinking. For example, rather than five or six academic periods, 45 minutes in length per day, Central Park East has two courses—one on the humanities and one on sciences and math—each lasting about 2 hours and co-taught by two teachers. The structure makes it possible for the teachers to teach 40 students during a day, rather than the 150 students per day in the typical secondary school. Not surprisingly, the teachers and students come to know one another well.

Another New York City school, the Urban Academy, facilitates teacher, student, and administrator collaboration in the way that it organizes office space. It spurns the convention of providing teachers and administrators a lounge and separate offices and instead chooses to provide for the dozen teachers (the administrators also teach) desks in one large classroom where the students also have their lockers. What the teachers lose in privacy, they gain by having multiple opportunities to informally meet with students, check with other teachers regarding a student's progress, or collaborate with teachers and students on a project.

The courses themselves typically focus on one or more "essential question," that is, questions to which there are no agreed upon answers and require students to use a variety of resources. For example, in the first year that I became acquainted with Central Park East, the question for the year was: What is a revolution? This led students to analyze political, industrial, and cultural revolutions and to ask open-ended questions, such as, Was either Malcolm X or Martin Luther King Jr. a revolutionary?

By focusing on one question for an extended period of time, students are pushed to develop what the school calls five major "intellectual habits": concern for evidence (how do you know that?), viewpoint (who said that and why?), cause and effect (what led to it and what else happened?), hypothesizing (what if, supposing that) and, most important, who cares? (Meier, 1995, p. 41).

Some of the Consortium Schools require students to carry out a year-long senior project. At Rochester's School Without Walls, seniors are required to propose a project, carry it out, and then defend their project in a committee meeting in much the same way that doctoral students carry out and defend dissertations. One student, David Waingarten, for whom I served on his committee as the "community representative," developed a video documentary on Hilton, a rural community near Rochester. He began by taking courses on documentary filmmaking at local universities and then researched the history of Hilton, focusing in part on the 1970s fire that destroyed the village center. He interviewed some of the residents involved in fighting the fire and collected film and photos from those at the fire, including video taken by television reporters. He then edited his film, wrote and dubbed the narrative, and composed and played the background music. Many residents attended the premier of his 90-minute video, which he subsequently donated to the town historian. The film enabled Waingarten to obtain a position with Ken Burns, a well-known documentary filmmaker in the United States. The student subsequently decided that the best path to a career in film was not through a university, but by producing independent films (see his acclaimed film *Addison's Wall*); he is currently an independent filmmaker active on both coasts. While Waingarten's project is obviously atypical, it points out the possibility of what secondary students can do if given the time and the resources to pursue an in-depth, sophisticated project.

While neither Central Park East, nor the Urban Academy, nor School Without Walls has a particular academic theme (other than strong academic preparation), several other schools in New York City have specific themes and partner with various institutions to achieve them. One school I visited, the School for the Physical City, aims to "prepare and empower city youth to take care of and take charge of the city." The school collaborates with several other organizations, including "Cooper Union, a private, tuition-free arts, architecture, and engineering college geared toward the children of working people," and Outward Bound, which has an expeditionary character-building program (Rose, 1995, p. 211).

Mike Rose, in *Possible Lives: The Promise of Public Education in America* (1995), interviewed the principal of the School for the Physical City, who described how a small school with an innovative, integrated curriculum allowed him to think differently about learning. The principal describes the transition from focusing on exams to focusing on learning. He stated that he did not think he had "ever thought as clearly about what learning is. The big leap [is] between teachers learning in order to teach and then teachers knowing enough about learning in order to teach what they know" (p. 213).

Yet, in 1996, the newly appointed New York commissioner of education, Richard Mills, began implementing a requirement that every student in the state could only graduate from secondary school if they passed five Regents exams in math, science, English, U.S. history, and global studies. While on the surface this might seem reasonable—in fact, the commissioner repeatedly asserted just how reasonable it was—for innovative schools like the Consortium Schools the requirement would severely undermine their ability to engage students in in-depth, interdisciplinary projects. Furthermore, the testing requirement undermined student academic success at all schools and increased the achievement gap between white students and students of color.

RAISING OR LOWERING STANDARDS?
NEW YORK'S HIGH-STAKES TESTING

As with all the reforms initiated by either states or the federal government since *A Nation at Risk*, New York State education officials promoted testing, accountability, markets, and choice by arguing that within an increasingly competitive global economy, such reforms were necessary to ensure that all students and the nation succeed. Moreover, they linked the discourse of the necessity of increasing educational and economic productivity with the discourses of decreasing educational inequality and improving assessment objectivity, a strategy also used by the proponents of No Child Left Behind.

Beginning in the 1990s, the New York State Board of Regents and the commissioner of education radically overhauled the education system by implementing standards and standardized testing, making graduation contingent on passing five statewide standardized exams, and requiring secondary students to enroll in only the state-regulated Regents courses, therefore eliminating locally developed and non-Regents courses (even International Baccalaureate courses) as a route to graduation.

While new testing requirements were being developed, the state also passed legislation promoting the establishment of up to one hundred charter schools—schools usually administered by for-profit educational corporations—which would take students and funds from the public schools.

The state's educational policymakers, including the former Chancellor of Education Carl Hayden and the present Commissioner of Education Richard Mills, justify the testing and accountability regime on the grounds that standards and standardized testing are the only way to ensure that all students, including students of color and those living in poverty, have an opportunity to learn. They argue that it is these same students who, because of the end of industrialization and the rise of globalization, can no longer be permitted to fail. All students must succeed educationally to ensure that the individual and the nation succeed economically.

Carl Hayden, the New York chancellor of education from 1996–2002 and recently nominated by Governor Spitzer to serve as the new State University of New York (SUNY) board chairman (Matthews, 2007), reflects these views in a letter:

> The requirement that *every* child be brought to a Regents level of performance is revolutionary. It is a powerful lever for education equity. It is changing for the better the life prospects of millions of young people, particularly poor and minority children who in the past would have been relegated to a low standards path. Too often, these children emerged from school without the skills and knowledge needed for success in an increasingly complex economy. (Hayden, 2001, p. 1)

Furthermore, Chancellor Hayden and Commissioner Mills argue that the curriculum standards were objectively determined and that standardized tests provide a valid and reliable means of assessing student learning. Such objective methods are required, they state, because teachers and administrators cannot be trusted to assess student learning objectively and accurately. Therefore, teacher-generated assessment protocols and instruments, such as those used by the Consortium Schools, are dismissed within this discourse as subjective and unreliable. Testing proponents imply that to adopt other means of assessment results automatically in a lowering of standards, as can be seen in Chancellor Hayden's (2001) response to the possibility of retaining the kinds of performance assessments used by the Consortium Schools:

> There is an even greater danger. The least rigorous, the least valid, the least reliable approved alternative [assessment] is then available to any school. Which schools will be first in the race to the lowest common denominator? Those having the most trouble bringing all children to a Regents level of performance. Those keen to reacquire the low standard option lost when the RCT [Regents Competency Test for the previously existing non-Regents track] and the local diploma were abolished. Those that never believed that all children can reach high standards. Were this to occur, it is all too apparent that poor and minority children would disproportionately bear the burden of diminished expectations. (p. 2)

However, the reforms have not resulted in more objective assessments. Almost every recent standardized exam given in New York State has been criticized for having poorly constructed, misleading, or erroneous questions, or for using a grading scale that either overstates or understates students' learning. Critics argue that an exam's degree of difficulty has varied depending on whether the State Education Department wants to increase the graduation rate, and therefore makes the exam easier, or wants to appear rigorous and tough, and therefore makes the exam more difficult. The pass rate for the exam can be increased or decreased simply by adjusting the cut score, turning a low percentage of correct answers into a pass or a high percentage of correct answers into a failure. In exams that students are likely to take as part of their graduation requirement, the State Education Department makes it easier for students to pass by lowering the cut score. This occurred, for example, in a recent Living Environments exam, where students only needed to answer 39 percent of the questions correctly to earn a passing grade of 55 percent (Cala,

2003). Conversely, the exams for the advanced, nonrequired courses, such as physics and chemistry, have been made more difficult. In a recent physics exam, 39 percent of students failed, in order, critics charge, to make Regents testing appear more rigorous. However, because primarily academically successful middle-class students take physics, the students and their parents were able to politically pressure the State Education Department to change the scoring (Winerip. 2003).

Furthermore, sometimes an unusually low or high failure rate may not be intentional but the result of incompetence. The June 2003 Regents Math A exam (the test students are most likely to take to meet the Regents' math requirement) was so poorly constructed that the test scores had to be discarded. Only 37 percent of the students passed statewide (Arenson, 2003). At Rochester's Wilson Magnet High School, a school ranked forty-ninth in the nation by *Newsweek*, primarily because of its IB Programme, all three hundred students who took the exam failed (Rivera, 2003). The Coalition for Common Sense in Education, an organization of parents, students, and educators, which I helped start, has repeatedly requested that the Department of Education release any validation studies conducted on New York's standardized tests. If such studies have been conducted, their results have never been made public.

The State Education Department has also been criticized for how it constructs the test questions. For example, a recent English exam received national censure for removing from literary passages references "to race, religion, ethnicity, sex, nudity, alcohol, even the mildest profanity and just about anything that might offend someone for some reason" (Kleinfield, 2002, p. 1). Examples of changes included deleting all references to Judaism in an excerpt from a work by Isaac Singer, and the racial references in Anne Dillard's description of the insights she gained when, as a child, she visited a library in the black section of town.

Many of the authors whose passages were changed were outraged that such changes occurred without their permission and substantially changed the meaning of the texts. Others pointed out the absurdity of having students answer questions that often referred to deleted portions of the text and objected that students might become confused if they were already familiar with the passage and were now confronted with the passage in which the meaning had been changed (Kleinfield, 2002).

Moreover, education inequality has increased as a result of the reforms. Quantitative evidence from New York State suggests that high-stakes testing has harmed education achievement. First, fewer students, especially students of color and students with disabilities, are completing high school. From 1998 to 2000, the number of students dropping out increased by 17 percent. A recent report for the Harvard Center for Civil Rights concluded that New York State now has the lowest graduation rate of any state for African American (35%) and Latino/a (31%) students (Orfield et al., 2004). In New York City only 38 percent of *all* students graduate on time, the fifth worst of the one hundred largest cities in the nation (Winter, 2004). According to another recent study, New York's graduation rate ranks forty-fifth in the nation (Haney, 2003). The tests also have negatively affected English-language learners, who were the highest diploma-earning minority in 1996 and the highest dropout minority in 2002 (Monk, Sipple & Killeen, 2001). Lastly, dropouts among students with disabilities have increased from 7,200 in 1996 to 9,200 in 2001.

In addition, while one of the State Department of Education's rationales for requiring Regents exams—eliminating the dual system where some students were tracked into courses with lower expectations—made sense, tracking has reemerged through other means. In the past, students advantaged by class or race were more likely to be in the Regents track while students of color and/or living in poverty were more likely to enroll in the typically less challenging local diploma. However, in most schools, unequal tracking continued as those who had taken Regents courses in the past now enroll in Honors and Advanced Placement courses and the Regents courses were made easier so that the students now enrolled in them would be able to pass. The Consortium Schools, which neither tracked students nor had low expectations, would have to enroll students in the less-challenging Regents courses.

In June 2005, the New York State legislature, in response to demands from parents and educators, pressured the Regents and the commissioner to lower the number of Regents exams, from five to two (one each in math and English), that Consortium School students would need to pass in order to graduate. However, students in all remaining schools in the state must still pass five Regents exams in order to graduate.

New York State's high-stakes testing has resulted in increasing inequality between advantaged and disadvantaged students. Similar high-stakes testing "reforms" have been implemented in some dozen other states and, complemented by the requirements of No Child Left Behind, result in simplified curriculum taught via teacher-directed pedagogy (Amrein & Berliner, 2002). High-stakes testing and accountability has lowered standards.

TEXAS: THE FOUNDATION FOR NCLB

Texas was one of the first states to implement high-stakes testing and George W. Bush, as ex-governor of Texas, used the "Texas miracle" to argue for NCLB and made Rodney Paige, superintendent of the Houston Independent School District, his first secretary of education. However, data show that the "miracle" in Texas was more likely a mirage that may have caused more harm than good. Even Texas legislators seem to realize the limitations of high-stakes testing as both the Senate and the House have recently passed bills to phase out the high-stakes aspects of the exam and, instead, to have the exam count as part of students' course grade. Such a reform makes is possible for students to fail the exam but still pass the course if they do well enough on the classroom assessments. In this section, I provide a brief overview of the Texas reforms, including some of the evidence showing that high-stakes testing was not contributing to greater student learning, improved accountability, or closing the achievement gap.

In 1984, the Texas legislature mandated changes in the statewide testing program, including, for the first time, making graduation contingent on students passing examinations in English and math. In 1990, regulations were passed making high school graduation contingent on passing more difficult "criterion-referenced" tests in math, reading, and writing. Reading and math assessments were also added for grades three through eight. Moreover, the test scores were used to hold schools and school districts accountable for students' learning, with schools rated for their performance. Test scores were not the only basis for determining school and district ratings. Secondary schools were also rated on the percentage of students graduating, putting pressure on schools to avoid students dropping out of school. Schools that received high ratings were eligible for cash awards and those that received low ratings faced sanctions, including possible closure (Haney, 2000). These examinations, the Texas Assessment of Academic Skills (TAAS), were first fully implemented under the administration of then-governor George W. Bush.

McNeil (2000) provides qualitative evidence for how the emphasis on tests and test scores undermined exemplary schools and teachers in Houston, Texas. She originally sought to understand why the schools were successful at educating working-class students. In the course of her research, the Texas standardized testing requirements (TAAS) were implemented and, as a result, she ended up documenting how previously successful schools began to expect *less* of their students as they prepared them to use the more basic skills required to pass the tests. For example, rather than teaching students to write well, teachers taught students to write the five-paragraph essay with five sentences in each paragraph that would receive passing grades on the standardized tests. In contrast to culturally advantaged middle- and upper-class students who might be seen as already possessing the skills required to pass the exams, disadvantaged students were seen as needing explicit drilling in writing five-paragraph essays. Unfortunately, learning to write five-sentence, five-paragraph essays does not transfer well to literacy required beyond the test and outside of school. Therefore, while already advantaged students tended to receive complex instruction, disadvantaged students did not and were likely to fall further behind. When schools expect less of disadvantaged students, they fall further behind.

But lowered expectations are not the only problem. Schools emphasizing test preparation are likely to devote most of their curriculum budget to test-prep materials rather than the enriched resources students need. In focusing on test preparation, schools are likely to reduce or eliminate subjects that are not being tested, including the arts and sciences. In Texas, during the years in which science was not tested in the early grades, science was rarely taught.

Lastly, rather than ensuring that more students do well, the pressure on schools and districts to raise test scores encourages schools to force weak students out before they take the required exam, and therefore reduce the risk that academically weak students would decrease the school's passing rate. In Texas, urban students are more likely to be retained in school, especially in ninth grade, the year before the required TAAS exam is first given. Students who are repeatedly retained are likely to give up and drop out of school. Haney (2000), in his study of the Texas education reforms, concludes that for the year 1996/1997, 17.8 percent of students were being retained in ninth grade (24.2% of African American and 25.9% of Hispanic students) and that only 57.57 percent of African American and 52.11 percent of Hispanic ninth-grade students were in twelfth grade four years later (Part 5, pp. 8–9).

However, schools in Texas face a double-edged sword: While forcing students out of school can raise test scores, they face possible sanctions for high dropout rates. Paige, as superintendent of the Houston Independent School District, resolved this dilemma by ordering principals to not list a student as dropping out, but as having left for another school (or some category other than "dropout"). Such creative recordkeeping resulted in the district claiming a significantly reduced dropout rate of 1.5 percent in 2001/2002 (and winning awards for excellence).

Eventually critics claimed that the dropout rate was covered up and subsequent research has revealed the rate to be much higher. Robert Kimball, assistant principal at one of the Houston high schools, raised questions when his school amazingly reported no dropouts even though its freshman class of 1,000 had dwindled to 300 by the senior year. A state investigation into sixteen high schools revealed that of 5,000 students who left school, 2,999 students should have been reported as dropouts but were not (Winerip, 2003). Significantly, Kimball adds, "Almost all of the students that were being pushed out were at-risk students and minorities" (Capellaro, 2004).

A second way to increase test scores is to increase the number of students classified with learning disabilities. While students in special education must take the TAAS, their scores are not included in those reported by the school. If students whose scores might negatively affect the overall school score can be excluded by placing them into special education, we might expect, after TAAS was implemented, the percentage of students in special education to increase. Haney shows that for the first four years in which TAAS was implemented, the percentage of special education students increased from 4.5 percent to 7.1 percent.

Given the ways in which the test scores have been manipulated by retaining students in grade, forcing students out of school, classifying more students into special education, and teaching to the test, one might expect the percentage of students passing the tests to increase—and indeed, the state reports that the percentage passing the TAAS exam has increased, the differences between the mean test scores for white, African American, and Hispanic students have decreased, and school dropout rates have declined.

Furthermore, even as schools have manipulated the scores by controlling who takes the exams, the higher average score may only mean that the students are performing better on the tests, not that they are learning more. While students' scores on the TAAS exam have been increasing, their scores on nationally administered tests, such as the university admissions exams, have been decreasing. Researchers investigating explained:

> The discrepancy in performance has a lot to do with the differences in the tests. TAAS was designed to make sure that students learned at least the basics of the state curriculum. The [university admissions tests], on the other hand, assess students on advanced academic skills needed for college. (Markley, 2004, A-1)

Therefore, Haney concludes, the Texas "miracle" was really a "mirage." Test scores have increased at the cost of educating all students and teaching students the basic skills required by the TAAS exam, rather than the complex skills required by postsecondary education and life beyond high school.

NO CHILD LEFT BEHIND

No Child Left Behind (NCLB) passed with large majorities in both the Senate (87–10) and the House (381–41), and was signed into law by President Bush on January 8, 2002. Like states that have adopted high-stakes testing and accountability requirements, such as New York and Texas, advocates for NCLB have promoted the reforms as necessary under globalization to increase efficiency, accountability, fairness, and equality. Almost all of these themes are encapsulated in Rodney Paige's (Bush's first secretary of education) description of how NCLB will increase our educational efficiency, ensuring that all children will learn, and closing the achievement gap between the United States and other countries. Paige, in response to an Organisation of Economic and Co-operative Development report, said:

> This report documents how little we receive in return for our national investment. This report also reminds us that we are battling two achievement gaps. One is between those being served well by our system and those being left behind. The other is between the U.S. and many of our higher achieving friends around the world. By closing the first gap, we will close the second. (Education Review, 2003)

A second component of neoliberal discourse focuses on standardized testing as a means of providing both a "quality indicator" to the consumer and "objective assessments" of student learning within education markets. In *No Child Left Behind: A Parents Guide* (U.S. Department of Education, 2003a), parents are told that standardized tests are a valid and reliable means of assessing students' learning, superior to teacher-generated assessments. The *Guide* advises parents that NCLB "will give them objective data" through standardized testing (p. 12). Further, objective data from tests are necessary because "many parents have children who are getting straight As, but find out too late that their child is not prepared for college. That's just one reason why NCLB gives parents objective data about how their children are doing" (p. 12). Teachers, NCLB strongly implies, have not rigorously enforced standards nor accurately assessed students, therefore covering up their own and their students' failures. Further, test scores are useful to parents because "parents will know how well learning is occurring in their child's class. They will know information on how their child is progressing compared to other children" (p. 9). Because teachers, NCLB claims, have relied too often on their own assessments, standardized test scores will also benefit them. NCLB "provides teachers with independent information about each child's strengths and weaknesses. With this knowledge, teachers can craft lessons to make sure each student meets or exceeds standards" (p. 9).

Standardized testing is promoted as a means of assessing the quality of students, teachers, and schools, thus ensuring that all children are treated fairly. Such a sentiment is reflected in Bush's recent statement that NCLB prevents "children from being shuffled through our schools without understanding whether or not they can read and write and add and subtract. . . . That's unfair to the children" (U.S. Department of Education, 2006c, p 3).

Because standardized testing ostensibly provides educators with objective information about students' learning and enables families to choose schools that are successfully educating children, NCLB supports a third central discourse in neoliberal efforts to transform education. Neoliberal reforms are touted for improving educational opportunities for all students and closing the achievement gap between white students and students of color. Paige, who as an African American lends credibility to these claims, argued that NCLB improves education for all children, especially African Americans.

We have an educational emergency in the United States of America. Nationally, blacks score lower on reading and math tests than their white peers. But it doesn't have to be that way. We need to collectively focus our attention on the problem. . . . We have to make sure that every single child gets our best attention. We also need to help African-American parents understand how this historic new education law can specifically help them and their children. (U.S. Department of Education, 2003b)

On other occasions, Paige explicitly connected NCLB to the civil rights movement of the 1960s, building on the legacy of Martin Luther King Jr.:

Forty-four years ago, Dr. Martin Luther King Jr. said, "The great challenge facing the nation today is to solve segregation and discrimination and bring into full realization the ideas and dreams of our democracy." The No Child Left Behind Act does that. The law creates the conditions of equitable access to education for all children. It brings us a step closer to the promise of our constitution. It fulfills the mandate in *Brown v. Board of Education*. It honors the trust parents place in our schools and teachers, with a quality education for all children, every single one. (Paige & Jackson, 2004)

But, whether NCLB and similar reforms emphasizing high-stakes exams and accountability were actually designed to increase fairness and equality can be questioned. First, both neoliberal and neoconservative organizations have stated that their real goal is to use testing and accountability to portray public schools as failing and to push for privatizing education provided through competitive markets. Second, evidence suggests that our educational system is becoming more, not less, unequal with a higher dropout rate for students of color and students living in poverty, who are also more likely to be subjected to curricula and pedagogical practices that are less demanding, such as Success for All and America's Choice.

UNDERMINING PUBLIC EDUCATION AND
PROMOTING MARKETS AND PRIVATIZATION

For many neoliberals the ultimate goal of the recent reforms is to convert the educational system into markets and, as much as possible, privatize educational services (Johnson & Salle, 2004). Organizations including the Manhattan Institute for Public Policy Research, the Heritage Foundation, the Fordham Foundation, the Hoover Institution, and the Milton & Rose D. Friedman Foundations have attacked public schools and teachers with the goal of replacing public education with private education. For many of them, vouchers and charter schools are the first step toward privatizing schools. For example, Milton Friedman, in *Public Schools: Make Them Private* (1995), advocated vouchers as a way "to transition from a government to a market system." Friedman states:

> Our elementary and secondary education system needs to be totally restructured. Such a reconstruction can be achieved only by privatizing a major segment of the educational system—i.e. by enabling a private, for-profit industry to develop that will provide a wide variety of learning opportunities and offer effective competition to public schools. (cited in Johnson & Salle, 2004, p. 8)

Johnson and Salle (2004) detail the concerted efforts by neoliberals and neoconservatives to attack public schools as "government schools." Since their publication, those attacks have continued. For example, neoliberal pontificator Jonah Goldberg's (2007) recent op-ed piece agrees with Friedman, stating that "Friedman noted long ago that the government is bad at providing services—that's why he wanted public schools to be called 'government schools'—but that it's good at writing checks. So why not cut checks so they can send their kids to [private, parochial, and charter] schools" (p. 12-A). He adds:

> One of the surest ways to leave a kid "behind" is to hand him over to the government. Americans want universal education, just as they want universally safe food. But nobody believes that the government should run all the restaurants, farms and supermarkets. Why should it run the vast majority of the schools—particularly when it gets terrible results? (12-A)

Others call for the immediate elimination of public education. Richard Eberling (2000), president of the Foundation for Economic Education, in *It's Time to Put Public Education Behind Us*, writes:

> It's time, therefore, to rethink the entire idea of public schooling in America. It's time to consider whether it would be better to completely privatize the entire

educational process from kindergarten through the Ph.D. . . . The tax dollars left in the hands of the citizenry would then be available for families to use directly to pay for their child's education. The free market would supply an infinitely diverse range of educational vehicles for everyone. (cited in Johnson & Salle, 2004, p. 8)

Some privatization advocates specifically anticipate that the high number of schools designated as failing to make adequate yearly progress (AYP) will lead to calls for privatizing schools. Howard Fuller, founder of the provoucher organization Black Alliance for Educational Options (BAEO), in a 2002 interview with the National Governors Association, said: "Hopefully, in years to come the [NCLB] law will be amended to allow families to choose private schools as well as public schools" (cited in Miner, 2004, p. 11).

The Bush administration has provided both policy and monetary support to privatization efforts. A voucher program was initially included in NCLB but removed when members of both political parties objected (DeBray, 2006, p. 87). Failing to include vouchers in NCLB, the administration imposed a $50 million experimental voucher program on Washington, D.C., over objections from residents and the U.S. Congress and granted $77.6 million to groups dedicated to privatization through voucher programs (Bracey, 2004). As we enter the early stages of reauthorizing NCLB, the Bush administration has again proposed that vouchers be part of the solution to improving public education, proposing $250 million for vouchers, called "promise scholarships," in the education budget for fiscal year 2008 (Klein, A., 2007, p. 25).

Privatization also plays a role in other aspects of NCLB. Schools failing to achieve AYP lose federal funding for tutors. Instead, tutoring is provided by for-profit and nonprofit community organizations, some of which have religious affiliations. The U.S. Department of Education earmarked $2.5 billion for private-sector tutoring in 2005/2006. But one analysis concludes that many corporations did not have a "viable business plan" and that there is great difficulty in providing private tutoring services (Borja, 2006, p. 5). Furthermore, schools face the prospect of having their administrations taken over by outside private for-profit organizations, such as the Edison Corporation.

Moreover, the administration has not been shy about supporting charter schools. The president and administrators in the Department of Education frequently use public appearances to promote charter schools as a solution to public school problems. In press conferences, when Paige defended NCLB, he also spoke out for largely unpopular charter schools (Shaw, 2004). At a conference I attended in spring 2004 on the relationship between the environment and human health, the Department of Education's director of interagency affairs exclaimed that he "knew nothing about education or science" and then devoted his talk to the virtues of charter schools, citing as evidence an unnamed report that he had not yet read.

Most tellingly, after Hurricane Katrina, the Bush administration and the Louisiana Department of Education replaced most of the New Orleans public schools with charter schools. First, they put all of the Orleans Parish public school employees on forced leave without pay; then, they voted to fire all the employees (Dingerson, 2006). As described in the publication *Dismantling a Community* (Center for Community Change, 2006):

> Over the past twelve months, buoyed by the support of the federal government, a network of conservative anti-government activists have moved with singular intensity to patch together a new vision for K-12 education that they hope will become a national model.
>
> It is a vision that disdains the public sector and those who work within it. It is a vision based on competition and economic markets. It is a vision of private hands spending public funds.
>
> Most disturbing, it is a vision that casts families and students as "customers," who shop for schools in isolation from—and even in competition with—their neighbors. It is a vision that, like the game of musical chairs, requires someone to be left without a seat. (p. 1)

Reed (2006) recently placed the transformation of schools and other public services in New Orleans within the context of the neoliberal project:

> The goal of this change is acceptance, as the unquestioned order of things, that private is always better than public, and that the main functions of government are to enhance opportunities for the investor class and suppress wages for everyone else. (p. 26)

The push for markets, choice, and competition have become dominant in policymaking. Robertson (2000) notes that proponents of choice and markets argue that "efficiency and equity in education can only be addressed through 'choice' and where family or individuals are constructed as the customers of educational services" (p. 174). Thrupp and Willmott add that by "the mid-1990s . . . the market solution (to just about everything) currently holds politicians in thrall" in the United States and elsewhere (Thrupp & Willmott, 2003, p. 13).

Furthermore, as indicated in *No Child Left Behind: A Parents Guide*, standardized testing and privatization are promoted as required given the incompetence of public school teachers. Teachers are blamed for the failures of the educational system. If teachers just had higher standards and more honest assessments, students would learn more (which ignores test data that shows that until recently, on average, students had been learning more each successive year).

However, blaming teachers for perceived educational failures should not be a surprise given the neoliberal and the Bush administration's antipathy toward unions. For neoliberals, unions are antidemocratic because they undermine individualism, in particular, the right of each person to negotiate in the workplace his or her own labor contract. Worse yet, teachers' unions also advocate for more social spending, not only for education but also for health care and other social services, and tend to vote for Democrats. Therefore, if possible, teachers' unions should be eliminated.

Understanding the neoliberal viewpoint regarding unions makes comprehensible Secretary of Education Paige's labeling the National Education Association (NEA) a terrorist organization when they objected to some aspects of NCLB. While Paige may have overreached in this instance and claimed he was misquoted, neoliberals, neoconservatives, and the Bush administration have specifically aimed to discredit teachers' unions. Johnson and Salle (2004) provide detailed evidence of the organized attack on teachers' unions, citing for example:

> You cannot understand the plight of America's public schools without understanding the force that exercises the most power over them. No, it's not the PTA. The strongest players in the schoolhouse game are the two teachers' unions, the National Education Association (NEA) and the American Federation of Teachers (AFT). . . . Increasing the welfare state, not improving children's education, is uppermost on this [NEA and AFT] agenda. . . . Despite their rhetoric, the

NEA and AFT routinely sabotage efforts for meaningful reform. In particular, the unions have mounted formidable opposition to school vouchers, privatization, and similar market-oriented reforms within the public system. . . . The unions say "efficiency," "competition," "productivity," and "accountability" would hurt children. Nonsense. The NEA and AFT are merely protecting themselves at the expense of children. (Haar, 1996)

The teachers' unions were completely marginalized in the formation of the Elementary and Secondary Education Act that led to NCLB (DeBray, 2006). The current Secretary of Education Margaret Spellings wants to reauthorize NCLB so that teachers' contracts can be broken in order to set up charter schools (Paley, 2007). Educators, under neoliberal policies, are merely the provider of services determined by others.

Lastly, NCLB requires that students, schools, and school districts be held accountable using the state's standardized tests, tests like those in New York that are poorly written, and whose results are often manipulated for political gain, often to make the commissioner of education look good and teachers look bad. However, even if the tests were well constructed and valid, the yardstick by which schools are measured—AYP—often discriminates against schools serving students of color and/or living in poverty.

The determination of whether a school is making AYP tells us little about whether a school is improving. Not only can we question the validity of the tests, but also the determination of success or failure may have little to do with whether the school is improving. Under NCLB, every state, with the approval of the federal Department of Education, determines, for every test, what knowledge and skills students need in order to demonstrate proficiency. States can, therefore, make achieving proficiency more or less difficult. However, for all states and every school, all students (regardless of ability or proficiency in the English language) are required to achieve proficiency by the year 2014.

However, contrary to a commonsense interpretation of AYP, schools are not evaluated on whether their test scores are improving, but whether their aggregated and disaggregated test scores exceed a minimum yearly threshold that gradually increases over the next decade. Consequently, a school is considered to be passing as long as its scores exceed the threshold, even if its scores fall. Similarly, schools that begin with initially low test scores may be considered failing even if they significantly improve their test scores, as long as those scores remain below the threshold. Therefore, achieving AYP may have nothing to do with whether a school's test scores rise or fall; achieving AYP depends only on exceeding the minimum threshold.

Furthermore, test scores strongly correlate with a student's family income; a school's score is more likely to reflect its students' average family income than teaching or the curriculum. As a result, the largest percentage of failing schools in New York can be found in poor, urban school districts. Almost all (83%) of the failing schools are located in the big five urban districts: New York City, Buffalo, Rochester, Syracuse, and Yonkers (NYSSBA, 2002). Most of the remaining failing schools can be found in smaller urban districts. The failure rate among schools in large urban districts is high, particularly at the middle school level. In Rochester, for example, all of the middle schools failed, which led Superintendent Manuel Rivera to fold all of the middle schools into grades seven–twelve schools, temporarily averting penalties for failing to meet AYP.

Because of the pressure to raise test scores, particularly in the urban school districts, teachers are compelled to teach the skills and knowledge that will be tested, neglecting more complex aspects of the subject and, indeed, some subjects altogether. Lipman (2004), in her ethnographic study of schools in Chicago, documents how testing requirements undermined the critical literacy goals of a bilingual school and frustrated creative, dedicated teachers. She describes how teachers at an elementary school, with a student population that was over 90 percent Mexican American, had to shift their focus away from using the students' own culture to develop critical literacy, and focus instead on test preparation. One teacher stated that she devoted the first half of the school year to developing students' writing skills and familiarity with sophisticated literature, but then, for the third quarter, shifted to test preparation. Test preparation includes getting students "used to the format of a short, mediocre selection of writing . . . to get them to recognize this type of question is asking you for some really basic information you can go back to look for" (Lipman, 2004, p. 110–111). The teachers, Lipman writes, experience "the contradictions and conflicts . . . between their efforts to help students see knowledge as a tool to analyze the world and the process and practice of preparing for standardized tests" (111).

Under accountability systems where schools are evaluated based on the percentage of students passing the standardized exams, it becomes rational to leave the lowest-performing students behind. In Chicago, as in England (Gillborn & Youdell, 2000), administrators instruct teachers to put their efforts into raising the test scores of those students who are closest to passing the standardized tests. As one teacher said:

> They tell us . . . "We don't want high kids and we don't want the lowest kids, we want the kids that are just about to pass the IOWA [standardized] test." So here you have a third or a fourth of your classroom really needs help to be ready for that next grade level and they don't get to go. (Lipman, 2004, 82)

Such educational triage exacerbates educational inequality as the students who either pass or are close to passing the test become valued commodities and those students who need the most help are left to fend for themselves.

Advocates for NCLB claim that working to improve test scores will result in improved student learning. Yet, in New York, students are subjected to tests that are badly written and scored to yield the results the commissioner of education desires. In both New York and Texas, students are retained and in other ways pressured to drop out to increase the overall percentage of students taking and passing the tests. In Chicago and elsewhere, students who are close to passing the exam or achieving proficiency (called "bubble kids") are provided extra academic attention while those deemed too far away from the goal are given little or no attention (Gilborn & Youdell, 2000).

As NCLB nears it reauthorization date, backers tout its "successes." In April 2006, Secretary of Education Spellings stated: "This law is helping us learn about what works in our schools. And clearly, high standards and accountability are working. Over the last five years, our 9-year-olds have made more progress in reading than in the previous 28 combined" (U.S. Department of Education, 2006a). Spellings (2006b) cites NAEP test scores showing a 7 percent gain from the period of 1999–2004 to support her claim. In response, critics such as Bracey (2006) point out that no NAEP data was gathered in the first two years (and we do not know that is not when the gain occurred), and that NCLB was in effect for a little more than a year before the 2004 testing, hardly enough time to take credit for any increase in reading test scores for nine-year-olds in that time. Furthermore, if the 2004 scores are compared to 1980, the increase is only 4 percent. Spellings chose to compare the 2004 test scores to a previous low point. Furthermore, she only refers to the gains in

scores among nine-year-olds, not mentioning that in the same period there
was no gain for twelve-year-olds and a decline of three points for seventeen-
year-olds (Bracey, 2006, pp. 151–152).

The Bush administration claimed that standardized tests, accountability,
tutoring services, and privatized education would increase students' test
scores. The Bush administration also claimed that NCLB would close the
achievement gap between white students, and African American and Hispanic
students. A recent study by the Harvard Civil Rights Project examined reading and math results by race on the NAEP before and after the implementation of NCLB (Lee, 2006). Orfield (2006) summarized the study concluding
that under NCLB:

> Neither a significant rise in achievement, nor closure of the racial achievement
> gap is being achieved. Small early gains in math have reverted to the preexisting
> pattern. If that is true, all the pressure and sanctions have, so far, been in vain or
> even counterproductive. . . . On the issue of closing the gap for minority and
> poor children, a central goal of NCLB, there are also no significant changes since
> NCLB was enacted. (pp. 5–6)

Further, market systems like NCLB restrict democratic debate over which subjects are valued and when and what kind of assessments are to be made. *No
Child Left Behind: A Parents Guide* (2003) boasts that NCLB will transform
schooling through testing and accountability. The authors state, "what you
value, you measure" (U.S. Department of Education, 2003a, p. 15). Because
the Department of Education measures math, reading, and science (but not
other subjects), they have stipulated which subjects are significant. Moreover,
they redefine literacy as reading, restricting funds for literacy instruction to
the teaching of phonics, vocabulary, and comprehension—programs evaluated through "scientifically controlled studies (like clinical trials)" (2003, p.
18–19).

Under NCLB, the federal and state governments make most of the significant educational decisions. Individuals are cast as consumers who can choose
among the choices provided by an educational marketplace. But for Young
(2000) and others, a strong civil society is necessary so that state power can be
limited and government held accountable to the public (p. 159). Under NCLB,
civil society is weakened and is held accountable by the government rather
than the other way around.

NCLB, then, is part of a larger political process in which concerns about increasing global economic competition have been a pretext for neoliberal reforms that focus on increasing efficiency through privatization, markets, and competition. Fairclough (2006) describes this process as one in which globalization is "hijacked in the service of particular national and corporate interests" (p. 8). Consequently, I have critiqued NCLB on two levels. It has failed to provide objective assessments, to improve learning, and to close the achievement gap. I have also situated NCLB with its more implicit, less frequently stated goal of promoting neoliberal solutions to societal problems.

To illustrate these points, I have provided data from a few states and recent analyses of the NAEP scores (Lee, 2006; Bracey, 2006). I strongly suggest that the exams used to assess schools have increased the number of high school dropouts. They have not made curricula more rigorous, nor have they closed the achievement gap; indeed, they are doing the opposite. What we need instead, as Darling-Hammond argued (2006) in a Distinguished Lecture at the annual American Educational Research Association Conference, is to remedy the "inequalities in spending, class sizes, textbooks, computers, facilities, curriculum offerings, and access to qualified teachers" (p. 13).

Furthermore, NCLB promotes the view that like other neoliberal reforms, we have no choice but to submit to the discipline of the market, rather than relying on processes of deliberative democracy. In the next chapter, I turn to describing, with Pauline Lipman as coauthor, the neoliberal reforms in Chicago and show why they might be considered as examples of "actually existing neoliberalism." Then, in the final chapter, I turn to proposing democratic alternatives to the neoliberal vision.

Renaissance 2010: The Reassertion of Ruling-Class Power through Neoliberal Policies in Chicago

David Hursh and Pauline Lipman

So far, I have shown how neoliberal political theory increasingly influences education policies. However, this chapter, using research on Chicago undertaken by Pauline Lipman and colleagues in Chicago, focuses on how neoliberal economic and education policies have been incorporating in a major city. By focusing on Chicago as an example of "actually existing neoliberalism" (Brenner & Theodore, 2002), we demonstrate that neoliberal theory differs from neoliberal practice: While neoliberalism is promoted as an efficient, politically neutral system beneficial for all, in Chicago it is creating an increasingly economically and spatially separate city. Consequently, people of color, those relegated to low-paying jobs, and progressive educators are beginning to contest neoliberal policies.

Over the last several decades, the Commercial Club of Chicago (hereafter Commercial Club) has taken an increasingly larger role in reforming the Chicago Public Schools (CPS). The Commercial Club, established in the 1800s to promote the interests of Chicago's corporate elite, has long influenced Chicago's education policies (see Wrigley, 1982; Shipps, 2006). However, with the publication of *A Nation at Risk* in 1983, the Commercial Club became central to making economic and educational policy. Its 1984 long-term strategic plan, *Make No Little Plans: Jobs for Metropolitan Chicago*, called for making Chicago a leading financial services center and upgrading the skills of workers (Lipman, 2003, p. 61). More recently, with Renaissance 2010 (here-after Ren2010), the Commercial Club began not only to make education policy central but also to oversee its everyday operation. The Commercial Club gained control over Chicago's public schools through the Renaissance Schools Fund (originally called New Schools for Chicago), a board appointed by the Commer-cial Club and composed of leading corporate representatives and "civic leaders" including the CPS's CEO and the president of the Chicago Board of Education. Referred to in the press as a "secret cabinet," this unelected body not only partic-ipates in the selection and evaluation of new schools, but also distributes Com-mercial Club funds to those schools (Rossi, 2004; Cholo, 2005).

Ren2010 includes not only remaking the public schools but the city itself and is part of a larger project to raze low-income African American commu-nities with the goal of gentrifying areas with new condominiums, luxury apartments, and retail services. Ren2010 reveals the increasing ability of the corporations to reshape both the city and schools in their own interests, using neoliberal education and economic policies to recreate Chicago as a global city central to the financial, real estate, retail, and service industries (see Lip-man & Haines, 2007).

In this chapter, therefore, we situate Chicago's Ren2010 reforms in the con-text of the neoliberal agenda, with the aim of revealing how Ren2010 fits within neoliberal ideology. In particular we show how neoliberalism asserts that societies function best when individuals make decisions within competi-tive markets rather than having governmental organizations or other agencies make decisions for them. The government that governs best is that which gov-erns least. Consequently, as I have shown, proponents of policies such as NCLB argue that current educational practices are wasteful and inefficient be-cause curricular and pedagogical decisions are made by school boards and teacher unions rather than in response to what parents find attractive in choosing a school for their child. Furthermore, social policy should promote economic growth by eliminating restrictions on corporate investment and growth, including reducing corporate taxes and regulations, and educating citizens to be productive employees. Social institutions, such as schools, exist to promote economic growth. Lastly, providing the conditions for corporate and economic growth will result in the improved economic conditions for all, therefore increasing equality (Olssen, Codd & O'Neill, 2004; Faux, 2006; Lauder et al., 2006).

However, as we will show, how neoliberalism works in practice differs from its theoretical assertions. As Harvey (2005), Ball (2003), and others have shown, "actually existing neoliberalism" (Brenner & Theodore, 2005) reflects neither in practice nor outcome what it claims to achieve in theory. Contrary to the illusion that markets regulate themselves, the conversion of education into a market system requires the intervention of the state for both the destruction of the existing institutional arrangements and political compromises and the creation of a new infrastructure. In Chicago, Ren2010 has undermined democratic decision making as parents, elected Local School Councils (LSCs), and community groups have less influence on the decisions that affect their lives. Recent educational and economic reforms in Chicago demonstrate how neoliberalism is not a natural or neutral evolution of political thought but instead provides, as Harvey (2005) writes:

> a benevolent mask of wonderful-sounding words like freedom, liberty, choice, and rights, to hide the grim realities of the restoration or reconstitution of naked class power, locally as well as transnationally, but most particularly in the main financial centers of global capitalism. (p. 119)

Moreover, as others have demonstrated, "neoliberal political practice has generated pervasive market failures, new forms of social polarization, a dramatic intensification of uneven spatial development at all spatial scales" (Brenner & Theodore, 2005, p. 5). We argue that, contrary to its claims, Chicago's recent neoliberal policies promote corporate and governmental intervention into daily life, and exacerbate already shameful inequalities. Urban policies, such as Chicago's, "mobilize city space as an arena both for market-oriented economic growth and for elite consumption practices" (Brenner & Theodore, 2005, p. 21), while at the same time securing order and control among low-income people of color. However, neoliberalism is not instituted without resistance, as working-class communities, particularly communities of color, struggle to resist neoliberal restructuring projects.

As I argued in chapter 4, neoliberalism aims to extend classical liberalism that emerged in the seventeenth century and to restore some of the power of the ruling class lost during the rise of social democratic liberalism in the middle of the twentieth century. Contrary to the "benevolent mask" in which neoliberalism is promoted as desirable, inevitable, and neutral, neoliberals aim to roll back gains in the right to social security, education, and welfare that were won over the last century.

In this chapter, we begin by briefly describing the research methodology in Chicago where Lipman and her colleague Nathan Haines[1] engaged in both archival research and progressive social activism. We then turn to describing and analyzing Ren2010 itself, with the aim of showing how neoliberal theory differs from "actually existing practice," and assert that education and economic reforms focused on choice, privatization, and the transformation of Chicago into a "global city" lead to the "class conquest of the city" by the middle and upper-middle classes (Smith, 2002). Moreover, because Chicago's educational reforms arise out of and parallel current school accountability policies, Ren2010 provides an example of how education policies, such as NCLB, lead to the privatization of public education. However, such policies also have the potential to provoke broad-based opposition. The Chicago case suggests that education may increasingly become a focus of democratic social struggles.

THE STUDY: METHODOLOGY

This chapter is grounded in multiple data sources: archival data, participant observation, and direct engagement in social activism. We align ourselves with a tradition of activist scholarship that values participation *with* communities, attention to the social analysis of groups experiencing oppression, and linking research, social action, and social movements (Carr & Kemmis, 1986; see also Fine et al., 2005). From July 2004 to August 2005 Lipman and her colleague Nathan Haines attended and participated in numerous school board meetings, public hearings, picket lines, community and school meetings, rallies, press conferences, planning sessions, coalition meetings, and forums. From August 2005 to May 2006, Lipman continued this work. Over three years, Lipman has had ongoing conversations with parents, students, teachers, school-level administrators, community organization leaders and members, members and heads of local school councils, the director and staff of a citywide parent organization, congressional staff, representatives of teacher and school employee unions, school reform organizations, and community-based research groups. Based on consistent involvement in these events, Lipman and Haines, and then Lipman, generated field and interview notes and collected documents that inform this account. Lipman has also been studying and writing about Chicago school policy for the past eight years (see Lipman & Gutstein, 2001; Lipman, 2002; 2003; 2004; Lipman & Haines, 2007) and this chapter is informed by that body of work. It also draws on recent policy chapters and documents of civic elites and community and labor organizations, media accounts, City of Chicago housing data, and relevant CPS and Illinois School Board of Education quantitative data. In addition, Lipman and Haines have volunteered as researchers for and with community organizations opposing Ren2010. Finally, Lipman has given public testimony about Chicago school policy at meetings and community forums related to Ren2010 throughout the city. These forums are also a rich source of data. The analyses developed into an evolving spiral of research/action, data analysis, and writing (Carr & Kemmis, 1986) in dialogue with the participants.

CHICAGO: NEOLIBERAL POLITICS IN A GLOBAL CITY

Chicago's transformation can be understood in the context of its drive to be a "global city"—a command center of the global economy (Sassen, 1994; 2004). During the past twenty-five years, Chicago has been transformed from an industrial hub to a corporate, financial, and tourism center. Successive city governments have concentrated public resources and local legislation to facilitate downtown development and gentrification of working-class and low-income neighborhoods, dramatically transforming the urban landscape (Lipman, 2004). The neoliberal strategy powering Chicago's economic development provides a clear example of the larger trend in urban economies. Moreover, Chicago bears watching as it has been a harbinger of national trends in education policy. Most notably, Chicago's 1995 school reform based on high-stakes testing and accountability provided a model for the 2001 No Child Left Behind (NCLB) federal education legislation.

On June 24, 2004, Andrew J. McKenna, chairman of the Civic Committee of the Commercial Club, declared that "Chicago is taking the lead across the nation in remaking urban education. No other major city has launched such an ambitious public school choice agenda." McKenna was referring to Mayor Richard M. Daley's announcement of Renaissance 2010. The plan would radically transform public education in Chicago by introducing markets into education, shifting control away from elected school councils and toward the unelected Commercial Club, and substantially reducing the power of the teachers' and other school employees' unions. It is fitting that the plan was announced at an event hosted by the Commercial Club. A year earlier, the Club's Civic Committee issued *Left Behind*, a report that called for the "creation of at least 100 public charter schools that increase parental choice and put meaningful competitive pressure on chronically failing neighborhood schools" (Civic Committee, 2004).

The Chicago Board of Education (Chicago Public Schools' governing body appointed by the mayor) passed Renaissance 2010 on September 22, 2004. Although the first stage of school closings associated with Ren2010 has affected particular neighborhoods, the plan is to overhaul a large part of the school system (Bluestein, 2005). The plan, as unveiled thus far, will close at least sixty Chicago public schools and open one hundred new schools: one-third charter schools and one-third contract schools (both run by outside vendors contracted by CPS) and one-third CPS "performance schools" (public schools subject to Ren2010 funding and policies). In fact, most of the new schools so far are charter or contract schools. For example, the Chicago Public Schools website lists thirteen new Renaissance 2010 schools opening in fall 2006; eleven are charter or contract schools (http://www.ren2010.cps.k12.il.us/). Ren2010 schools have five-year performance contracts with CPS. In exchange for this increased accountability, the school district promises greater flexibility in curriculum, instruction, and school organization (CPS Policy Manual, 2004, p. 4). In the Civic Committee report (*Left Behind*, 2003) and in the school system's official press releases and public statements, flexibility and innovation are linked to freedom from union contracts and elimination of elected Local School Councils (LSCs).[2]

Renaissance 2010 institutionalizes corporate control of public schools. Final selection and approval of Ren2010 schools rests with the CEO of CPS. However, the Commercial Club, in exchange for agreeing to help fund the project by raising $50 million, was granted increased power over the education system through the Renaissance Schools Fund, an organization composed of leading corporate representatives, civic leaders, as well as the president of the Chicago Board of Education and the CEO of Chicago Public Schools. This unelected body participates in the selection and evaluation of Ren2010 schools, while distributing Commercial Club funds for which the schools must compete (Field, 2005). School enrollment policy is also murky and leaves room for formal and informal selection processes.[3]

Since Ren2010 was announced in June 2004, it has provoked public controversy and community resistance not seen in relation to Chicago Public School policy over the past fifteen years. Central to the public discussions and media accounts are issues of educational equity, class inequalities in the city, race, gentrification, community participation, education quality, and the role of teachers' unions. CPS leaders, the mayor, and the Commercial Club contend that Ren2010 will create "options" and "choice," promote innovation, and raise achievement by introducing competition, reducing the power of teachers' unions, creating more efficient school governance, and opening up mixed-income schools in mixed-income communities. On the other hand, opponents claim the plan will accelerate gentrification, destabilize schools by increasing student mobility, harm low-income and homeless children in particular, eliminate community participation, weaken unions, and privatize education (Midsouth Fact Sheet, n.d.; Chicagoans United for Education press conference, July 1, 2005).

FROM EDUCATION ACCOUNTABILITY TO PRIVATIZATION

By situating Ren2010 within the history of Chicago school reform, in particular the 1988 and 1995 reforms, we can understand how it both builds upon the past and reverses recent efforts to empower parents, teachers, and other community members. It also reflects the more than century-long involvement of the corporate elite in the Chicago schools through the Commercial Club and exemplifies the increased corporate control of schooling under the neoliberal turn. Lastly, it mirrors the national and global neoliberal agenda.

The 1988 Chicago school reform both decentralized and centralized school governance. It established the Local School Councils, elected local school governing bodies composed primarily of parents and community members. Although known nationally as the most extensive institutionalized form of democratic community participation in local school governance, the 1988 law also centralized oversight of school finances in the corporate-dominated School Finance Authority. Ren2010 eliminates Local School Councils while further centralizing power.

Chicago's 1995 school reforms installed an education policy regime based on high-stakes accountability. Under the centralized control of the Chicago Public Schools administration, students and schools were labeled and classified based on test scores, and thousands of "failing" students were retained in their grade, prevented from graduating eighth grade, and sent to remedial basic skills high school programs while hundreds of schools were put on probation and a few were reconstituted altogether with new principals and teaching staffs (Lipman, 2004). At least initially, the policies appealed to a broad common sense that something must be done to address the widespread failure of the schools to educate African American, Latino, and low-income students in particular (e.g., Orfield, 1990). Persistently high dropout rates, failure rates, and low reading and math levels are indicators of deeper inequities in what is taught, how it is taught, and who has access to what kinds of knowledge (see Newmann, Bryk & Nagaoka, 2001).

Despite a stringent system of sanctions for failure, these educational outcomes have not changed much since the policies were established. The policies did little to rectify significant inequities in resources and opportunity to learn between selective schools and schools in affluent neighborhoods and the majority of schools serving a district that is more than 90 percent students of color and 85 percent low-income. Nor did centralized mandates for improvement address underlying ideological issues, inequitable curricula, and disconnections between the curriculum and students' cultures, communities, and the strengths they bring to school—factors at the core of the failure of schools to educate low-income children of color.

What the accountability regime did accomplish, intentionally or not, was a system of ranking school failure that established a necessary condition to identify schools to be closed under Ren2010. Teachers, administrators, and community members opposed to Ren2010 argue that the accountability system also created a cycle of changing central mandates and overseers of local schools that is destabilizing and demoralizing for school staff. This compounded the historical failure to invest adequate resources in low-income schools. A community leader testifying before the Board of Education summed up the connection between this recent and long-term history and the current plan to close schools: "You can't separate the failure in these schools from what's been done to them by CPS" (School Board meeting, 2004, September 22).

Ren2010 provides neither more funding for schools nor support for teachers but rather aims to improve schools by restructuring them as a private-public ventures and by introducing markets and competition, therefore ostensibly improving efficiency. As we will show, charter schools, as well as contract schools formed through Ren2010, are rooted in neoliberal economic rationality. They further open schools to corporations for investment and profit; they support markets as a solution to all problems, and, in the process, undermine collective processes of democracy, such as the LSCs, by promoting democracy as individual choice.

Furthermore, charter schools and other reforms promoted under Ren2010 intersect and complement national, global, and local neoliberal agendas. No Child Left Behind (NCLB) provides both impetus and opportunity to implement a neoliberal education agenda in Chicago. Under NCLB, schools that persistently fail to meet ever-increasing test score benchmarks are subject to having their "operations" turned over "to a private company" approved by the Department of Education or restructured and reopened as a charter school (U.S. Department of Education, 2002, p. 7). In addition, both schools and school districts that fail to meet test score benchmarks are subject to takeover by the states.[4] *Left Behind* contends that to avert state action, which would undermine Chicago's efforts to position itself as a global city, "NCLB has made the need for choice more transparent" (Civic Committee, 2003, p. 55). Moreover, Chicago, like other districts, realizes that closing schools and reopening them as "new" schools restarts the clock on meeting adequate yearly progress (AYP) requirements and postpones the sanctions imposed under NCLB.

Moreover, charter schools, as public-private partnerships, form an opening wedge into the public education sector as a source of direct capital accumulation without full responsibility for running a city's school system.[5] Charter schools work by "shaving off" aspects of the education system to private providers (Robertson & Dale, 2003). Roger Dale (1989/1990) notes that "before education can be brought into the marketplace and made subject to consumer choice, a range of possible alternatives has to be created" (p. 9). This function is served by the creation of charter and contract schools resulting in a mixed public-private system of school choice. Although some progressive community organizations, groups of parents, and teachers frustrated with public schools have created culturally centered, innovative, and social justice–oriented charter schools, the neoliberal context favors business-oriented models (Wells et al., 2005). In Illinois (where Chicago is located), as in most states, charter schools are given less per-pupil public funding than public schools, and most of them have to use part of the state funding to cover costs of facilities.

These limited resources force many charter schools started by community organizations to contract out school administration to education management organization businesses or develop partnerships with business groups or corporations (Wells et al., 2005).

Charter schools, as well as contract schools formed through Ren2010, are rooted in neoliberal rationality that privately run schools can provide education more efficiently, and a system of school choice will spur innovation and raise quality, including within those public schools forced to compete with charters for students. These assumptions are partly grounded in the belief that the market allows rational economic individuals to make choices in their own interests. Under this logic, turning schools over to the market through choice of charter, contract, and public schools will give parents the freedom to pursue the best schools for their children. As Harvey (2005) points out, this logic assumes there are no asymmetries of power. In fact, "Better informed and more powerful players have an advantage that can all too easily be parlayed into procuring even better information and greater relative power" (p. 68). Stephen Ball's (2003) study of school choice in England revealed that middle-class families used their financial resources, expertise in the market, and their social and cultural capital to secure school advantages for their children.

The evidence from choice programs elsewhere (Whitty, Power & Halpin, 1998; Tomlinson, 2001; Hursh, 2005a) suggests that Ren2010's choice provisions are unlikely to improve schools for many working-class and low-income students and students of color, though they may attract and keep middle-class residents in the city. Whether school selection mechanisms are formal or informal, they can work against working-class students of color as they advantage middle-class students (Ball, 2003). An important result of choice policies has been more social class segregation in schools as choice allows them to be more selective in choosing their pupils. In the school marketplace, some students are regarded as "valuable commodities," while others are regarded as "undesirable." Tomlinson (2001) concludes that in Britain, the market system in education appears to create new disadvantages for "ethnic minority" students and their parents that outweigh advantages. Similarly, in Chicago, a public Montessori school created in an elementary school, which formerly served children living in a public housing project, now enrolls children of new middle-class residents of the gentrifying area while enrolling few children from the public housing development (Finkel, 2006).

RENAISSANCE 2010 AS NEOLIBERAL THEORY
AND ACTUAL EXISTING PRACTICE

Ren2010 not only promotes neoliberal education policy but also is part of a process of neoliberal restructuring of the urban economy and urban space. Not only does it establish a business climate in schools more conducive to capital by undermining unions and democratic public participation, but Ren2010 also reflects the way in which "cities have become strategically crucial geographic arenas in which a variety of neoliberal initiatives—along with closely intertwined strategies of crisis displacement and crisis management—have been articulated" (Brenner & Theodore, 2002, p. 351). According to Smith (2002), the neoliberal restructuring of cities indicates a move away from social democratic liberal urban policy to the "class conquest of urban policy" marked by (1) state subsidies of capital and direct involvement of capital in urban decision making, (2) withdrawal of the state from social reproduction, and (3) increased social control of low-income and working-class communities. Neoliberal urbanism is characterized by new forms of public-private partnership through which the state facilitates capital accumulation and public decision making by corporate/financial interests without any public accountability. Renaissance 2010 firmly establishes the neoliberal urban agenda.

While neoliberal theory emphasizes markets and competition, resulting in reduced governmental intervention into everyday life, and increased prosperity for all, Chicago's recent policies have increased corporate and governmental intervention into daily life and exacerbated economic, social, and spatial inequalities along lines of class, race, and ethnicity. Moreover, Chicago's neoliberal policies result in an increasingly dual city—one section taken over by the financial and upscale real estate, retail, and tourist interests and the other composed of the urban poor, who provide the services demanded by the privileged and who are to be safely contained within their neighborhoods.

However, these policies are contested and Ren2010 has become an arena in which working-class communities, particularly communities of color, struggle to resist neoliberal restructuring. Ren2010, then, can be examined not only for its specific policies but also to show how neoliberal theory differs from "actually existing practice," as well as to demonstrate that education and economic reforms focused on choice, privatization, and the transformation of Chicago into a "global city" enabled the middle and upper-class "class conquest of the city" (Smith, 2002).

It is not surprising that the Commercial Club, an organization of Chicago's most powerful corporate and financial interests, is a proponent of freeing public schools from public control and bringing them into the market. The Commercial Club's 58-page report, *Left Behind,* is an explicitly free market, anti-union, anti-democratic-control document. The report begins with data showing that scores on state standardized tests did not significantly improve from 1999 to 2002 despite major systemwide accountability reforms. It cautions that the school system's corporate leadership is not to blame: "It is essential to keep in mind that this failure [of CPS schools] is not attributable to the current CEO of the system or its board" (Civic Committee, 2003, p. 21). (Chicago has a corporate-dominated board of education appointed by the mayor.) Instead, the Commercial Club contends that the problem lies with parent participation in school governance and union regulations. The failure of the school system to improve is due to "the constraints of the city-wide teachers' union contract" and the inefficiency of Local School Councils (p. 51).

Echoing a long line of neoliberal critics of public education (e.g., Friedman, 1962; Chubb & Moe, 1990), *Left Behind* argues that the root cause of the problem is that public education is a "monopoly" that should be broken by turning schools over to the market, which can run them more efficiently and which will promote innovation: "Competition—which is the engine of American productivity generally—is the key to improved performance of our public schools" (Civic Committee, 2003, p. 55). The report's authors note that vouchers would be the "preferred" solution but because "the political climate in Illinois seems hostile," the best plan is to fund existing charter schools and work politically to expand their number. Mayor Daley's announcement of Ren2010 reiterated the Commercial Club's argument: "This model will generate competition and allow for innovation. It will bring in outside partners who want to get into the business of education. It offers the opportunity to break the mold. It gives parents more options and will shake up the system" (CPS, 2004, June 8).

Progress is equated with neoliberal market solutions that offer equity through market choices and quality through competition (see also Ball, 2003) and represents an ideological shift that promotes new thinking and new social relations, which are essential to the neoliberal project. For neoliberalism to succeed, writes Ball (2001), "It is not just a matter of introducing new structures and incentives but also it requires and brings about new relationships, cultures and values" (p. xxxii).

REN2010 AND THE ASCENDANCE OF CAPITAL IN URBAN GOVERNANCE

The Renaissance Schools Fund and Mayor Daley's advocacy for the Ren2010 plan capture the institutionalized fusion of corporate and state power. Ren2010 installs a powerful organized body of powerful corporate and financial elites as direct actors in shaping public school policy and directing its implementation. The Commercial Club proposed Ren2010, Mayor Daley announced it at a Commercial Club event, and the Commercial Club created the Renaissance Schools Fund (RSF), a public-private partnership at the highest level, to direct the plan. RSF includes the chairs of McDonald's Corporation and Northern Trust Bank, a partner in a leading corporate law firm, the CEO of Chicago Community Trust (a major local corporate/banking foundation), the retired chair of the Tribune Corporation, and top CPS officials. The Chicago Board of Education also appointed the former vice president of Bank One and CEO of the Chicago Board of Trade as chief administrative officer of CPS, a position for which he is paid one dollar per year. The strategy to sell Ren2010 (including the concept, administrative structure, "message," and "communications timing") to "stakeholders" and "opinion makers" was developed by a leading corporate consulting firm that claims to "provide a unique business perspective" and "thought leadership" to CPS leaders (Kearney, 2004). A central component of this plan is a model of neoliberal organization—a "franchised model" of less bureaucratically controlled schools run by "vendors" with a regional "business services center" that services "clients" (i.e., teachers and administrators) (Kearney, 2004).

Legitimizing corporate and financial actors to make crucial decisions about public education, without public accountability, is a neoliberal turn that goes beyond private operation of individual charter schools. It gives capital direct control over institutions of social reproduction financed through public funds. On a lesser scale, it parallels the takeover of New York City fiscal authority by banking and financial interests—a germinal event in the evolution of neoliberal urban governance (Harvey, 2005). The direct intervention of the Commercial Club reveals the strategic role that the city's school system plays in Chicago's neoliberal development strategy and in making Chicago a global city. *Metropolis 2020* (Johnson, 1998), the Commercial Club's proposal for

Chicago Metropolitan Region development, calls for improving school systems in order to prepare "employees who can, at the minimum, read instruction manuals, do basic math and communicate well," and to improve the school performance of "minorities" because of their expanded role in the area's economy (p. 6). These goals are driven by the intense global competition among metropolitan regions to attract production facilities, corporate headquarters, investment, and business services industries. But the city itself also requires schools of exceptional quality to attract high-paid professionals and managers. This is an explicit impetus for the creation of new college preparatory magnet schools in Chicago's upper-income and gentrifying areas (see Lipman, 2004).

Apple (2001) reminds us that for neoliberals, democracy is equated with the freedom to consume in the market, and the ideal of the citizen as purchaser. "Rather than democracy being a *political* concept, it is transformed into a wholly economic concept" through voucher and choice plans in education (p. 39, emphasis in original). This transformation masks the increased political power of capital to govern daily life. In the case of Ren2010, the power of capital is legitimated ideologically by the promotion of Ren2010 as a school choice plan and furthered materially through the elimination of Local School Councils (LSCs) as a form of democratic school governance. LSCs are elected community and teacher governance bodies in each school authorized to select the school principal and allocate the school's budget. Although the effectiveness and level of community participation in LSCs has been uneven, and has been eroded by greater centralized regulation through the accountability system, LSCs are nevertheless a form of institutionalized democratic participation by parents and community members in local schools (Katz, 1992; Katz, Fine & Simon, 1997; Bryk et al., 1998; Fung, 2004). LSCs have been under attack by school system leaders since Chicago's 1995 accountability reforms. Under Ren2010, LSCs will be eliminated in the charter and contract schools, which have private boards.

The significance of LSCs lies in their relative political power in the city. In a highly centralized, corporate-dominated city and aligned mayoral regime, they are one of very few democratically elected forums of democratic participation, and thus a means of grassroots organizing that can extend beyond the schools. In that sense they are a local arena within which low-income and working-class communities can contend for power around decisions that affect their daily lives. Some of their presidents and members, particularly on the African American South and West sides, have taken a leading role in the resistance to Ren2010. Eliminating LSCs undermines one of the few official bases of local community power in the face of the city's consolidated neoliberal agenda of downtown development, gentrification, and corporate and financial power (see Lipman, 2004). Ren2010 establishes the neoliberal preference for governance by experts and elites as a politically stabilizing environment for the free workings of the market (Harvey, 2005).

Renaissance 2010 also institutionalizes neoliberal economic and social relations within the city's public sector, weakening labor in favor of capital. The logic of the market favors cost-cutting by reducing labor costs and limiting educational services. Charters that reduce operating expenses (through, for example, lower wages for teachers and other school employees, limited services to special education and bilingual education students, fewer extracurricular options, and less experienced teachers) increase their profits. And those schools that focus on high-stakes standardized tests are more likely to succeed in the current policy context. Because charter school employees do not have union protections, they are subject to the same labor abuses, system of favoritism and cronyism, and lack of job security as nonunion workers are in other sectors. For example, at one Ren2010 charter school, teachers negotiate their salaries individually, are not allowed to leave the building during the school day, and have no job security from year to year. The weakening of teachers' and other school employees' unions is significant for trade unions in general. The Chicago Teachers Union, with more than 37,000 members, is one of the largest unions in the city. As Susan Robertson points out, charter schools have been one of the means the state has used to overcome opposition to neoliberal policy by breaking up existing unionized sectors (Robertson, 2003).

REN2010 AND GENTRIFICATION—THE
CLASS CONQUEST OF URBAN SPACE

Over the past twenty-five years, gentrification has moved from a marginal sector of urban economies to a pivotal strategy of urban development (Smith, 2002). Gentrification in the neoliberal context merges local, national, and transnational capital to create gentrification complexes of upscale housing, retail outlets, cultural attractions, streetscapes, and recreation and parks. It is facilitated and managed by a fusion of state and corporate power wielded through public-private partnerships and policies that use public funds for private development (see Smith, 2002). Lubricated by local government policies that favor and subsidize developers, gentrification "serves up the central and inner-city real estate markets as burgeoning sectors of productive capital investment" (Smith, 2002, p. 446). It is fundamentally about reconstituting urban space for the middle- and upper-middle-class consumers who are also a critical labor force at the center of global city functions (business services, advertising houses, legal firms, and so on) (Sassen, 2004).

A central theme in community meetings organized to protest Ren2010 is that the plan is linked to the displacement of low-income African Americans and gentrification of their communities. In fact, the evidence suggests that Ren2010 significantly extends the connection between education policy and gentrification that was apparent with the creation of six new selective magnet high schools begun in 1999 (Lipman, 2004). The schools that are being closed under Ren2010 are almost entirely in African American communities experiencing gentrification. We turn, therefore, to examining the relationship between Ren2010, school closings, and gentrification by looking at two Chicago communities: Englewood and the Midsouth.

In February 2005, CPS announced it was closing two elementary schools and the main high school in Englewood, an African American community on Chicago's South Side. Englewood is one of the most economically devastated areas of the city without even a grocery store. Yet Englewood is located near the expressway and public transportation and is described in local newspapers' Real Estate sections as the next "hot" neighborhood. A city Housing Department official noted, "There is a growing interest in Englewood these days" (Almaca, 2005, p. 1-1, 16A). Without any new housing in the area in years, Englewood, a community with a median household income of $18,955, is now the site of a new $150 million development to build 550 new single family homes costing $165,000 to $365,000 and a second development of 185 houses. A $250 million city investment includes a new police station and library, a $150 million community college campus, and a $22 million shopping district. At the same time, longtime residents are being driven out by increases in property taxes up to 80 percent and a 41 percent increase in house foreclosures in the past ten years.

The Midsouth was the initial focus of Ren2010 in 2004. In July 2004, the Midsouth Plan to close twenty of the twenty-two schools in this area was leaked to the press. People in the community immediately mobilized to fight it. In November 2004, after months of demonstrations, angry testimonies at school board meetings, and community hearings, the board bowed to community pressure and withdrew the plan, choosing instead to move much more cautiously in the Midsouth while planning school closings in other areas. Midsouth community members charged that the Midsouth Plan was designed to push them out of their neighborhood in order to further gentrification. In fact, the plan would have forced children to transfer to schools out of the community, which on top of the destruction of public housing, skyrocketing property taxes, and a severe lack of affordable housing, would be another incentive to leave the community. Looking more closely at the Midsouth situation illuminates the connection between school policy, gentrification, and neoliberal urbanism.

Gentrification of the Midsouth and Englewood can be understood by looking at economic and political forces shaping the city—specifically, the spatial dynamics of capitalism and the cultural politics of race. Writing on space as a constituent element of capitalism, David Harvey (2001) argues that capital attempts to resolve economic crises through the "spatial fix"—the creative destruction and reconstruction of investment in the built environment. "The inner contradictions of capitalism are expressed through the restless formation and re-formation of geographical landscapes" (p. 333). This process underlies gentrification (see Smith, 1996) and the Midsouth and Englewood provide clear examples. Hit hard by deindustrialization in the 1980s and into the 1990s, stable working-class African American families became low-income and unemployed, and both communities had some of the highest concentrations of poverty in the United States (Bennett, 2007; Venkatesh et al., 2004). During this period, landlords failed to maintain rental properties, allowing them to decline in value, and the state, through the Chicago Housing Authority (CHA), followed suit. The CHA failed to maintain public housing complexes, such as 28 high-rise buildings containing 4,321 public housing units in the Midsouth, to the point of rendering many of them uninhabitable, thus justifying their demolition (Popkin, Cunningham & Woodley, 2003). Under the Chicago Housing Authority Plan for Transformation (2000), demolition of 19,000 units of public housing in Chicago is almost completed. The land on which they stood, devalued through disinvestment, is now a source of lucrative reinvestment. In the case of the Midsouth, that land is near to Lake Michigan, major expressways, public transportation, and two public universities and is ten minutes from downtown Chicago. It is not surprising that the Midsouth is a focus of some of the most intense gentrification in the city (see Lipman & Haines, 2007).

Gentrification, as a pivotal strategy of capital accumulation in urban centers, is facilitated by the local state that provides public funds, tax abatements, and publicly financed infrastructure for development, amounting to a transfer of wealth to the capitalist class. Gentrification significantly depends on public funding. Mega developments in the Midsouth are examples. For instance, Michaels Development Company (a private development consortium with large projects in a number of U.S. cities) has a $600 million investment in Legends South, a complex of more than 2,300 houses and apartments on a two-mile stretch of land where the Robert Taylor Homes and Stateway Gardens public housing complexes stood. Its market advantage accrues from public subsidies. Seventy-seven percent of the financing for this privately owned development comes from public sources—federal, state, and city dollars. The developers also got the land free through a ninety-nine-year lease from the Chicago Housing Authority, and they received a $4.5 million tax increment financing subsidy (Handley, 2004, p. 3A) from the city. Michaels is just one of the mega investors in the Midsouth.

Mayor Daley and CPS officials argue that redevelopment will revitalize the area as a "mixed-income" community with "mixed-income" schools. Although described as mixed-income housing, much of the redevelopment on public housing land will be beyond the reach of working-class and low-income families. Legends South, a "mixed-income" development, will provide public housing for just 18.3 percent (our figure based on Venkatesh's analysis) of the former Robert Taylor residents (Venkatesh et al., 2004). As Neil Smith (2002) points out, "'Social balance' sounds like a good thing—who could be against social balance?—until one examines the neighborhoods targeted for 'regeneration,' whereupon it becomes clear that the strategy involves a major colonization by the middle and upper middle classes" (p. 445). There are winners and losers. With condominiums and townhouses in the Midsouth ranging from $175,000 for a one bedroom apartment to $500,000 homes, transformation of public schools in the area is crucial to attract middle-class buyers.

The Midsouth Plan was a school choice plan designed to appeal to the middle class. Students would no longer be assigned to a school based on where they lived. Instead, the region was to be divided into "expanded attendance areas," each of which would include three to five "innovative" school choices within walking or commuting distance (Bluestein, 2005, p. 49). Over 90 percent of the students who currently attended Midsouth schools are from low-income, African American families. However, the Midsouth Plan stated that schools would serve one-third middle-income, one-third moderate-income and one-third low-income students, and there was no guarantee that community residents would be able to attend specific schools. A Midsouth community organization said pointedly, "What happens to the other 2/3 low-income students? DISPLACEMENT" (Midsouth, n.d.).

As residents of Englewood and the Midsouth see signs of gentrification all around them, they contend that the new Ren2010 schools are not designed for them. In February 2005, at a meeting in a church in Englewood, community residents denounced the history of disinvestment in their schools and community and the gentrification and removal of low-income African Americans that is rampant in the Midsouth and now beginning in Englewood. One community member summarized the sentiment of the meeting: "They're pushing us out of the community under the guise of school reform." In community meetings and rallies in 2004 and 2005, community members took pains to argue that there were links between gentrification and Ren2010. Two years into the plan, that argument had become common in the analyses of the Chicago Teachers Union, other school employee unions, community organizations, and school reform groups. This collective sense is grounded in the rapid pace and geographical extension of gentrification, lack of affordable housing in the city, and movement of low-income African Americans to inner-ring south suburbs of Chicago (Minding the Gap, 2003). From 1980 to 2000, the number of concentrated low-income tracts declined in the city (due to gentrification) while they increased in the suburbs (Chicago Metropolis 2020, 2001, p. 35).

RACIALIZATION OF NEOLIBERAL POLICY

Chicago exemplifies the centrality of race in the neoliberal urban agenda. The justifications underpinning the withdrawal of the state from social reproduction and the intensification of social control are highly racialized. Neoliberal calls for individual responsibility and social discipline reference the putative social pathologies of African Americans that must be corrected or contained by social policy (Bonilla-Silva, 2001). The representation of gentrification as benevolent rests on depicting the city as an "urban frontier" and areas to be gentrified as needing to be "tamed" (Smith, 1996). Specifically, the path to gentrifying African American communities is paved by their construction in media and public discourse as spaces of social pathology that must be cleaned out and reconstructed through the infusion of middle-class role models. Neglected for decades, the neighborhoods and schools are then identified as the problem to be fixed through the presumed authority of the (white) middle class (Bennett, 1998). A recent *Chicago Tribune Magazine* study on the "rebirthing" of the Midsouth reiterates this theme. "As drug trafficking, street crimes, and other negatives have ebbed in the community, its focus has shifted from cleaning out bad elements to bringing in beneficial ones" (Grossman & Leroux, 2006). This discourse is rooted in historically persistent white supremacist urban mythology "that has identified Blacks with disorder and danger in the city" (Haymes, 1996, p. 4). This association is repeated in the discourse about black urban schools that are defined as "failing," on "probation," and characterized by lack of student and teacher effort (Lipman, 2004). This was made explicit when the CEO of CPS defended the closing of Englewood High School by declaring that the school, 100 percent African American, exhibited "a culture of failure."

Just as disinvestment produced decline in public housing and led to calls for its demolition, disinvestment in schools serving African American and Latino children has become an argument for closing them. At the same time, the accountability system has provided the tools to demarcate the schools to be closed. Like other major U.S. cities, it is a truism that problems in schools in low-income African American sections of Chicago are intertwined with the lack of jobs, decent affordable housing, and decayed physical infrastructure and have a history of racial segregation and lack of necessary resources (Orfield, 1990; Rivlin, 1992; Anyon, 2005). In Chicago, African American students comprise the majority of CPS enrollment and historically have had the lowest test scores, were more likely than any other racial/ethnic group to be retained under CPS accountability policies, and, of the 147 elementary schools put on probation from 1996 to 2001, 75 percent were African American (Bryk, 2003). Chicago Public Schools have failed to invest the substantial resources and make the fundamental curricular, pedagogical, and structural changes that would be necessary to redress the sedimented inequities and injustices that plague public schools serving African Americans. Indeed, Lipman's field notes from school board meetings record consistent and urgent appeals by African American and Latino parents for repairs of school buildings and replacement of outdated textbooks and science labs. Instead, CPS has subjected schools in these communities to more external regulation and control (Lipman, 2004).

Before communities can become new sites of capital accumulation, they have to be devalued, prepared for development, and reimagined as places of value. Their "regeneration" is possible only through dispersing the people who live there, erasing the identities they have constructed for their communities, and replacing them with new, sanitized images. Thus, the Robert Taylor Homes pubic housing development becomes Legends South. Similarly, schools are closed and reopened with new identities. The neoliberal urban economic logic intersects with the racial logic of white supremacy to fuel real estate development and retake the city for the mostly white middle class. In the restructured economy, many African Americans have become an expendable labor force. In Chicago's global city image of middle-class stability, upscale leisure and cultural venues, and affluent housing and retail complexes, they are a presence to be excluded or contained (Smith, 1996; Parenti, 1999).

Stephen Gill (2003) argues that neoliberalism and resistance to it define the present social conjuncture. Despite claims to economic growth and individual freedom induced through the market, the reality of neoliberalism is increased inequality, social immiseration, and the suppression of democracy.

> The disjuncture between the ideology of self-regulating markets and the everyday reality of persistent economic stagnation—intensifying inequality, destructive interplace competition, and generalized social insecurity—has been particularly blatant in precisely those political-economic contexts in which neoliberal doctrines have been imposed most extensively. (Brenner & Theodore, 2002, p. 352)

As capital increasingly privatizes the public sphere, coerces communities into cooperating, and undermines the democratic process, possibilities for resistance arise. This dialectic unfolds at multiple scales and in specific contexts, including education. It is the possibilities for resistance to which we now turn and conclude.

RESISTANCE

The consequences of Ren2010 go far beyond education. They extend to the survival of African American communities, union jobs, wages and benefits; the quality of teachers' work and students' educational experiences; democratic community participation in local schools; affordable housing and the determination of who can live in Chicago. As a result, Ren2010 has provoked the beginnings of a broad-based resistance that includes teacher and other school employee unions, Local School Councils, a citywide parent organization, community organizations, school reformers, progressive teacher organizations, and advocates for homeless families. These social sectors have come together in a sometimes tenuous but nonetheless significant coalition that has succeeded in making Ren2010 a persistently contentious public issue. The resistance made Ren2010 a major topic at almost every Board of Education meeting during the 2004/2005 school year, and it is regularly covered in the local press. Despite CPS leaders' assertion of "real and widespread community support" (CPS, 2004, September 9), opposition mushroomed with community hearings, forums, angry testimony, and pickets at monthly Board meetings, a campout in front of the Board of Education building, door-to-door organizing, a student walkout, rallies, and press conferences. In the summer of 2005, school employee and teachers' unions, a progressive teachers' organization, school reform groups, community organizations, a citywide parent organization, and local school council federations formed a citywide coalition.

This opposition has won partial victories, blocked some school closings, and put public school officials and the mayor on the defensive as they are forced to try to explain and justify the plan to communities and in the press. What is instructive about this resistance is that it has forged new alliances across communities and social sectors that had not worked together. Although incipient, and tenuous, these alliances bridge racial and ethnic differences, geographic distances, unions and communities, professionals and grassroots activists. They are spawned by the sweeping political and economic agenda underlying Ren2010.

While the resistance specifically focuses on school closings, privatization, gentrification, and attacks on unions, running through it all is outrage at the dismissal of any meaningful participation by the communities and people affected by these policies. This is a consistent refrain in pubic meetings, in public statements, and in Lipman's interviews and ongoing conversations with the various social actors affected. Ren2010 was developed by public officials and corporate elites behind closed doors, with a plan to sell it to the public devised by a corporate consulting firm. There was no consultation with the community before deciding to close twenty of twenty-two schools in the Midsouth, schools in Englewood, and other low-income communities. In fact, teachers, principals, and community members sometimes found out that their school was closing through the newspaper. Over two years, there has been a consistent pattern of top-down decision making with no community consultation. CPS officials have devised, revised, and imposed each phase of Ren2010 without consulting teachers, principals, school employees, families, and communities of color about decisions that affect their lives and about which they have privileged knowledge (see, for example, Midsouth Fact Sheet). This blatant disregard and disrespect is perceived as racist and dictatorial.

However framed by those lined up against Ren2010, the contest is fundamentally political. It is about the suppression of democracy. Education reforms that blur the distinction between public and private interests establish the indirect political power of nonstate actors who "perform political functions under no effective political control" (Bonaventura de Sousa Santos quoted in Dale & Robertson, 2004, p. 153). In other words, the neoliberal project promises individual freedom and choice. In practice, the impoverishment and suffering it produces necessitate the constriction of democracy and, when necessary, increased surveillance, policing, and force (Wacquant, 2001; Gill 2003; Harvey 2005). The Ren2010 case reveals the face of coercive neoliberalism operating through the authoritarian state and a discourse of containment that delegitimizes democratic participation in school decision making. School officials denounce opponents of Ren2010 as irresponsible complainers "who don't want change" (Field notes CPS School Board Meeting, 8/25/04; 9/22/04). While powerful state and corporate actors concentrate political power through Ren2010, they negate the right of ordinary members of the public, particularly communities of color, to speak.

On a structural level, the privatization of schools and the replacement of LSCs with nonelected bodies eliminate democratic participation in decisions that govern public and publicly funded institutions. At their best, LSCs have been both a training ground and platform for local democracy—a context that has developed the capacities of community members and parents to participate in democratic governance. Some LSC members have emerged as significant community actors outside of schools. Without overstating the case, LSCs represent the potential for a "thick democracy" of direct community participation in decision making that directly counters the neoliberal model of governance (Gandin & Apple, 2003). By redistributing power to parents and community representatives, LSCs "asserted the capacity of ordinary citizens to reach intelligent decisions about educational policy" (Katz, 1992, p. 62). Negating the legitimacy of the community to speak on school issues and eliminating LSCs is therefore part of a process of redefining civic competence in order to concentrate the authority to make civic decisions in the hands of financial and professional elites.

As we write this chapter, the coalition opposing Ren2010 has achieved limited success. While forty-three of the fifty city councilpersons supported a resolution for a moratorium on further school closings until an independent study can be conducted on the multiple impacts on students and schools, the resolution was never brought to the floor of the city council. Although the future of this opposition movement and the outcome of Renaissance 2010 are uncertain, the resistance provides an example that education may become a focus of anti-neoliberal democratic social struggles. However, building solidarities across different groups and countering both the "common sense" of neoliberal discourse—choice is good and markets are fair—presents a major challenge.

NOTES

1. Lipman and Haines collaborated on research on Renaissance 2010 from July 2004 through August 2005 (see Lipman & Haines, 2007). Much of the research discussed in this chapter is based on their collaboration.

2. See for example: CPS press release, September 22, 2004.

3. Although, according to CPS policy (approved September 22, 2004), no more than 10 percent of the schools are to be selective enrollment magnet schools (selection by test scores and grades) and students are supposed to have the right to return to their old schools when they are reopened, the Board also reserved the right to establish other student assignment processes (CPS Policy Manual, 2004, p. 9).

4. Under NCLB, schools that do not make adequate yearly progress (AYP) for five years are subject to state takeover.

5. See K. Saltman's *The Edison Schools: Corporate Schooling and the Assault on Public Education.*

7

Imagining the Future: Alternatives to Neoliberalism and High-Stakes Testing

I entered teaching in the 1970s because, like John Dewey, I realized that it is in the classroom where we answer the perennial philosophical questions of what is worth knowing, whose knowledge should be in the curriculum, and the nature of the relationship between teacher and learner. I also hoped that education could contribute to creating a more socially just and inclusive society, one in which citizens contributed to the common good through debate, conversation, and action.

I continue to teach knowing that, over the last several decades, many of the ideas that I incorporated into my own elementary teaching in the 1970s—developing a community of learners in which students actively construct their understanding of the world using interdisciplinary problem-based learning and authentic assessments—are now supported by research (National Research Council, 1999, 2001) and practice. Dewey's progressive approaches, as incorporated in schools like my own and those that make up the Performance Assessment Consortium, work.

In spite of the efforts of educators, what we have learned about teaching and learning has been undermined by policies that have shifted control over schooling to first the state and then federal levels, with high-stakes testing increasingly determining what and how we teach. In addition, neoliberals aim to transform education into a market system in which teachers and schools compete with one another; and, when possible, they aim to privatize education.

The reforms in education are part of a larger neoliberal project to alter the relationship between the individual and government and the nature of democratic decision making. As Pauline Lipman and I described regarding Chicago, the corporate and political elite have taken control of the municipal government and education system with the aim of turning Chicago into a global city where profits can be sought through real estate, tourism, and retail business. In doing so, they have redirected government away from its historical social democratic obligation to provide for the common good toward developing economic and educational policies supporting the interests of the professional and managerial classes. In Chicago and elsewhere, the concept of the common good is replaced by individual responsibility and corporate welfare. As a result, cities like Chicago are becoming dual cities, separate and unequal, in which the children of the professional and managerial class attend schools offering Advanced Placement and International Baccalaureate courses that prepare them for leadership roles, and children of the working poor attend schools that teach the basic skills necessary to work in the service and retail industry. Neoliberal education policies may well achieve Snedden's goal of preparing students for "their probable futures."

Therefore, in this last chapter, I want to reassert the possibility of a society and schools that support community welfare and the public good over corporate profit, and propose how we might work toward those goals. First, we must resist the discourse that presents neoliberalism as inevitable. As I have argued and will expand upon in this chapter, neoliberals argue that because of globalization, we have no choice but to adopt neoliberal reforms and we must, therefore, implement economic policies emphasizing free trade, economic deregulation, and, in education, high-stakes testing, accountability, and markets. In response, I provide some of the evidence that neoliberalism falls short of achieving its own declared goals of providing greater economic growth and equality. Since the adoption of neoliberal policies, economic inequality has increased *within* countries, such as between the rich and the poor in the United States, and between countries, particularly *between* the global north and the global south.

Second, neoliberals' faith that societal decisions can best be made through individual market choices undermines our ability to confront social and environmental problems, such as rebuilding New Orleans (Klein, 2007; McLaren & Jaramillo, 2007), reducing global warming, or providing adequate health care. As Polanyi (1954) observed over fifty years ago, "To allow the market mechanism to be sole director of the fate of human beings and their natural environment, indeed, even of the amount and use of purchasing power, would result in the demolition of society" (p. 73). Because recounting all the ways in which neoliberalism damages human welfare and the environment would require a book, I focus on economic growth and inequality, President Bush's and China's environmental policies, and New Orleans after Hurricane Katrina (which has experienced what Noami Klein refers to as "disaster capitalism").

Third, I return one final time to briefly describe the effects of neoliberalism on schools, this time showing how neoliberal ideals of efficiency and privatization have negatively transformed the nature of schooling in New York City. I also describe how high-stakes testing has thwarted my own efforts to develop schools where teachers collaborate in implementing interdisciplinary curriculum in which students take a lead in the creation of knowledge.

Lastly, I conclude where I began, proposing what we might do to develop democratic schools and society. In particular, I argue that educators need to work with other educators and the wider society to combat neoliberal policies that undermine social justice in schools and society.

HIJACKING GLOBALIZATION TO SERVE NEOLIBERAL INTERESTS
In the same way that the Bush administration and other neoliberals and neoconservatives have used the fear of terrorism to promote a war on Iraq and to restrict civil liberties, they use the fear of losing jobs to economically competitive countries to promote high-stakes testing, accountability, markets, and privatization in schooling. As I have described, raising economic fears as a tactic to reform schools is not new. The National Association of Manufacturers blamed schools for the recession of 1893 and *A Nation at Risk* blamed schools for the recession of 1983. Blaming schools for our nation's economic problems diverts attention from examining needed changes in economic policies, such as placing a tax on international trade or the so-called Tobin Tax (see Tabb, 2002, pp. 212–250).

However, the current reforms differ in that they are embedded within a neoliberal logic favoring

competitiveness; decentralization, devolution, and attrition of political governance, deregulation and privatization of industry, land and public services [including schools]; and replacing welfare with 'workfarist' social policies. . . . A neoliberal subjectivity has emerged that normalizes the logic of individualism and entrepreneurialism, equating individual freedom with self-interested choices, making individuals responsible for their own well-being, and redefining citizens as consumers and clients. Margaret Thatcher's notorious 'there is no alternative' seems to be a self-fulfilling prophecy. (Leitner et al., 2007, pp. 1–2)

Neoliberals explicitly link an increasingly globalized world to the reforms they desire. Thomas Friedman, in *The Lexus and the Olive Tree* (1999), asserts that globalization requires free market capitalism:

The driving force behind globalization is free market capitalism—the more you let market forces rule and the more you open your economy to free trade and competition, the more efficient your economy will be. Globalization means the spread of free-market capitalism to virtually every country in the world. Therefore globalization also has its own set of economic rules—rules that revolve around opening, deregulating and privatizing your economy, in order to make it more competitive and attractive to foreign investment. (p. 9)

In his current best-selling book, *The World is Flat: A Brief History of the Twenty-first Century* (2005), Freidman raises the specter that the United States is losing jobs to other, primarily Asian, countries because our schools fail to teach students the required skills. Earlier, I quoted President Bush regarding his assessment of the "achievements" gained under NCLB, where he argued that because we live in a global world in which we compete with China and India, we have no choice but to implement the testing and accountability measures of NCLB.

The fear that the United States is losing the educational battle with China and India has become so dominant that it is rarely questioned. Gerald Bracey (2007), in his annual report on the state of the schools, cites several stories providing inflated figures for the number of engineers graduating from universities in China and India, including those in *Rising Above the Gathering Storm: Energizing and Employing America for a Bright Economic Future* (2006), a report from the prestigious National Academies.

Politicians and educators reinforce the fear over increasing numbers of Asian engineers. Senator Hillary Rodham Clinton (Young, 2007), campaigning in Iowa for president, stated: "We are not increasing the number of young people going into math and science. We're not turning out more engineers and researchers to compete with China and India" (2007). The National Center on Education and the Economy's reform proposal, *Tough Choices or Tough Times: The Report of the New Commission on the Skills of the American Workforce* (2007), similarly raises the fear of the increasing number of engineers in China and India and calls for educational reforms focusing on privatization, competition, and vocationalism. Rochester's newspaper, the *Democrat and Chronicle*, reported on a suburban school district's plan for a community discussion on Friedman's *The World is Flat* because, as a district administrator stated: "new technology has flattened the economic playing field around the globe and as a result, American students will need special skills to compete against workers in India, China, and other population centers" (McDermott, 2007).

Increasingly globalization, writes Fairclough (2006), has been hijacked "in the service of particular national and corporate interests" (p. 8), including neoliberal policies that aim to reduce social spending by introducing markets and privatizing services not only in education but also elsewhere, such as Social Security. Globalization has become a central or nodal discourse, around which other discourses cluster, such as the discourse of neoliberalism, the knowledge-based economy, and educational efficiency. These discourses form a network in which they support one another and as a network are more difficult to resist.

Furthermore, by presenting both globalization and neoliberalism as inevitable, they are presented as processes, writes Fairclough (2006),

> without human agents, in which change is nominalized ("globalization") . . . a process in a general and ill-defined present and without a history (it just is what it "is"), which is universal (or, precisely, global) in terms of place, and an inevitable process which must be responded to in particular ways—as "is," which imposes an "ought," or rather a must. (p. 45)

Consequently, observes Dean (2002), neoliberals can portray themselves as powerless to choose any other path.

> Those who use a discourse of economic globalization can simultaneously hold "there is little (or, at least, less) [they] can do to exercise national sovereignty"

and "it is imperative to engage in comprehensive reforms of the public sector, welfare, higher [and lower] education, finance, and labor market control. (p. 55)

While it is the case that manufacturing and service jobs are increasingly exported to China and India—purchasing goods not made in China is increasingly difficult—jobs are going to those countries not because the United States is not producing skilled workers, but because we cannot compete with the low wages in those countries. Within our current trading agreements, corporations, in order to earn a larger profit, export jobs to low-wage countries.

NEOLIBERALISM'S FAILURES AND CONTRADICTIONS

Rather than blaming schools for our economic problems, we need to examine neoliberal reforms. The neoliberal assertion that we can only increase the economic growth of the United States and the world by replacing the social democratic liberalism that was dominant after World War II with a neoliberal approach has been analyzed and found wanting. In this section I provide evidence that neoliberalism has not only failed to improve economic growth as much as previous social democratic approaches but also that neoliberalism diverts us from solving societal and educational problems by means other than instrumental calculations and, consequently, exacerbates problems. As I have demonstrated, recent educational reforms have not succeeded in closing the achievement gap nor improved overall student learning. Here I examine how neoliberalism has increased economic inequality, exacerbated ecological degradation, and consigned New Orleans to a dismal future.

David Harvey, in *A Brief History of Neoliberalism* (2005), reveals how neoliberalism is neither inevitable nor neutral, but instead is "the restoration . . . of naked class power" through "a benevolent mask full of wonderful-sounding words like freedom, liberty, choice, and rights" (p. 119). Neoliberalism promises that individuals pursuing their own economic self-interests will result in greater economic benefits for the whole society. But Stiglitz (2002), Harvey (2005), Faux (2006), and Jomo & Baudot (2007) detail how neoliberal policies instituted in both the United States and (through pressure from international financial organizations such as the World Trade Organization) the world have resulted in decreased economic growth and increased inequality.

Jeff Faux, in *The Global Class War* (2006), exposes the increasing economic disparity in the United States since the implementation of neoliberal policies.

The top one-tenth of 1 percent of income earners have more than doubled their average income in the past two decades, while the share going to the bottom 90 percent fell (pp. 68–69). Over that time, worker productivity increased while income remained the same. With falling wages, many families have only been able to improve their income by increasing the number of family members in the workforce and the number of hours worked.

Free trade, which is promoted as providing increased economic opportunity, often results in increased inequality. For example, the North American Free Trade Agreement (NAFTA) precipitated a crisis in the value of Mexico's peso, leading to its devaluation, fewer jobs, and higher living costs. Consequently, the poverty rate in Mexico increased from 45.6 percent in 1994 to 50.3 percent in 2000. Likewise, the poorest 40 percent of Mexicans earned 10.7 percent of the household income in 1994 and only 9.1 percent in 2000.

Joseph Stiglitz, past president of the World Bank and author of *Globalization and Its Discontents* (2002), describes how neoliberal policies have increased the disparity between the rich and the poor throughout the world. He particularly blames the International Monetary Fund for damaging the economies of less developed countries. Benjamin Friedman (2002), in reviewing Stiglitz's book, adds that twenty-one of the poorest fifty countries became poorer during the decade of the 1990s. Likewise, Harvey (2005) points out that the growth of the global gross national product declined under neoliberalism:

> Aggregate economic growth rate stood at 3.5% or so in the 1960s and even during the troubled 1970s fell only to 2.4%. But the subsequent growth rates of 1.4% and 1.1% for the 1980s and 1990s (and a rate that barely touches 1% since 2000) indicate that neoliberalism has broadly failed to simulate worldwide growth. (p. 154)

Consequently, the working and middle class of numerous countries, including Argentina, Brazil, Bolivia, Chile, and Venezuela, have revolted against the gap between neoliberal rhetoric—that all will benefit—and the realization that it has only benefited a small ruling class.

In the United States, economic inequality has increased, with the rich becoming richer and the poor becoming poorer. Beginning in the 1980s, "the wage gap between working and middle-class Blacks and Whites began to increase" and has continued to the present (Anyon, 2005, pp. 40–41). George

Bush's approval rating continues to decline as the public rebels against the administration's effort to cut taxes for the rich while reducing services for the poor. As Harvey (2005) writes, "neoliberalism is recognized as a failed utopian rhetoric masking a successful project for the restoration of ruling-class power" (p. 203).

Neoliberalism has not only not achieved its promised economic gains, but prioritizing profits over other nonmonetary aspects of our lives has been disastrous for the environment, especially after the election of George W. Bush, who has refused to endorse reductions in carbon emissions on the assertion that it might hinder economic growth (Bello, 2005, p. 183). In opting out of the Kyoto protocols, Bush claimed: "I will explain as clear as I can, today and every other chance I get, that we will not do anything that harms our economy. . . . That's my priority. I'm worried about the economy" (Bush, cited in McKibben, 2006, p. 18). Such policies have exacerbated global warming to such an extent that implementing carbon emission reductions now may be too late to halt continued melting of ice sheets in Greenland and Antarctica with the related rise in sea levels (Hansen, 2006).

The negative consequences of China's wholesale adoption of capitalist, neoliberal policies have become increasingly evident. Harvey (2005, p. 174) describes how neoliberal policies contributed to the degradation of China's environment. China now has sixteen of the twenty worst cities in the world with respect to air pollution (Bradsher, 2003) and, according to a recent study, has surpassed the United States as the top emitter of carbon dioxide (*New York Times*, 2007). Recent reports (Barboza, 2007) indicate that China's air and water pollution causes 750,000 premature deaths annually and costs $160 billion a year in damages. Furthermore, the drive for capitalist expansion at all costs has contributed to numerous ecological disasters (Yardley, 2004), including benzene and nitrozine spills in the Singhua River (Lague, 2005), which contaminated drinking water for millions of people, and the drive has led to exporting dangerous products, including toys with lead paint, defective auto tires, and poisoned toothpaste.

Even though it is Bush's and other neoliberals' unending faith in the market that has contributed to our environmental mess, they continue to resist governmental regulations of greenhouse gases or incentives for reducing energy use, and persist in believing that the market will create technological solutions to our environmental problems.

The neoliberal desire to implement market solutions and privatization wherever possible is visible in the Bush administration's response to the devastation caused by Hurricane Katrina in New Orleans and the Gulf Coast. The Bush administration has used the disaster as an opportunity to implement neoliberal policies in rebuilding housing, businesses, and the public schools. A Heritage Foundation (2005) publication describes rebuilding New Orleans as an opportunity to support free enterprise and made the following recommendations regarding rebuilding New Orleans:

> In general, tools such as tax credits and voucher programs, which allow individuals and families to direct funds, should be utilized to encourage private sector innovation and sensitivity to individual needs and preferences. . . .
>
> Private vision, not bureaucracy, must be the engine to rebuild. . . . The critical need now is to encourage investors and entrepreneurs to seek new opportunities within these cities. Bureaucrats cannot do that. (p. 1)

Subsequently, the Bush administration has collaborated with antigovernment activists to dismantle the public schools and the teachers' union, and replace them with private-administered charter schools. The nonprofit group Center for Community Change, working along with New Orleans public high school students, has examined the dismantling of the city's schools (Center for Community Change, 2006), concluding that neoliberal and neoconservative reformers distain

> the public sector and those who work within it. It is a vision of competition and economic markets. It is a vision of private hands spending public funds. Most disturbing, it is a vision that casts families and students as "customers," who shop for schools in isolation from—and even in competition with—their neighbors. It is a vision that, like the game of musical chairs, requires someone to be left without a seat. (p. 1)

Soon after the hurricane struck, the Bush administration began to work to replace the public schools with charter schools, first by waiving federal restrictions on charter schools and then granting $20.9 million to Louisiana for establishing charter schools. At about the same time, the Orleans Parish School Board placed the district's 7,500 employees on unpaid "Disaster Leave" (Center for Community Change, 2006, p. 10), and two months later all the employees were fired, leading to some of the teachers filing a lawsuit and gaining a temporary restraining order. After the retraining order expired, the board again voted to fire the teachers and later allowed the district contract with the teachers to expire. Most of the public schools began converting to charter schools, and by June all but four of the twenty-five public schools, helped by an additional $24 million grant from Secretary of Education Spellings, became charter schools (p. 28). Most of the charter schools did not open as scheduled and three schools operated by a California corporation had their charter revoked three weeks before opening day, leaving students without a school (p. 34).

Naomi Klein, in *The Shock Doctrine: The Rise of Disaster Capitalism* (2007), describes how neoliberal governments and corporations are using disasters such as Hurricane Katrina and the Boxing Day Tsunami to expand the power of private corporations and provide investment opportunities, while at the same time reducing or eliminating public housing, hospitals, social agencies, and schools. Adolf Reed also (2006) places the transformation of schools and other public services in New Orleans within the context of the neoliberal project. He wrote:

> The goal of this change is acceptance, as the unquestioned order of things, that private is always better than public, and that the main functions of government are to enhance the opportunities for the investor class and suppress wages for everyone else. (p. 26)

As in Chicago and New Orleans, New York City's public schools are being subjected to neoliberal reforms emphasizing high-stakes testing and accountability in which students are treated as raw material to be shaped into a finished product. And like Chicago, the mayor, Michael Bloomberg, using rights granted to him by the state legislature, chose the public school chancellor, replaced school board members, and eventually dissolved the school board (Hancock, 2007). Like other neoliberals, who believe in the business solution to everything, Bloomberg chose as chancellor Joel Klein, recent CEO for the global media giant Bertelsmann. Since becoming chancellor, Klein has employed the "tools of business—top-down decisions, marketplace incentives, and a belief in private sector solutions to public school problems" (Hancock, 2007, p. 16). Klein operates the schools as businesses, describing them as "key units" in which services such as professional development are contracted out, and schools compete with one another based on their quarterly test scores (p. 17). In addition to the high-stakes standardized tests already required by the state and federal governments, students are tested every few weeks, and must pass the end of the year tests to be promoted from the third, fourth, and seventh grades. Moreover, the schools have recently developed a program in which they will pay students for attendance and high test scores (Bosman, 2007).

All this fits into Chancellor Klein's social efficiency approach to education, where he "refers to children as cars in a shop, a collection of malfunctions to be adjusted. Teachers need to 'look under the hood,' he says, to figure out the origins of the pings" (Hancock, 2007, p. 20). Such diagnostic information, he claims, is provided by the multiple tests that contribute to "data-driven" instruction. Thomas Sobol, past New York commissioner of education and now professor emeritus at Teachers College, observed that Chancellor Klein's reforms "are preparing children to do these small tasks, stripping education down to its parched bones. The soul of education is left at the door" (Hancock, 2007, p. 21).

Furthermore, parents are concerned that they and the teachers have become disenfranchised as Klein has centralized power in his office and in the principals, many of whom he appointed. Neither the newly created Panel for Educational Policy (which replaced the School Board) nor the teachers' union has a voice in decision making. Sobol describes the concentration of power as part of the assumption that corporations know best and responds: "The arrogance, my God, of saying because we know how to run Kmart, we know how to educate children represents a giant defeat for democracy" (in Hancock, 2007, p. 17).

While the specifics of the education reforms in New York City, New Orleans, and Chicago differ, they all incorporate neoliberal notions of markets and privatization, as well as the increasing corporate model and role in making public welfare decisions. They also are similar in that most of the students in the school districts are students of color from working-class families who submit to "drill and kill test-prep curriculum," and whose families are marginalized in the political process. As Lipman and I point out regarding Chicago, this is very much a racialized process in which racial groups are removed from the political process. McLaren & Jaramillo (2007) observe that the responses to Hurricane Katrina raise "powerful questions about American democracy and the racial divide," and that we need a "deep democratic dialogue about poverty, racism, and the obligation of government," which has yet to occur (p. 6).

FIGHTING FOR DEMOCRATIC EDUCATION AND SOCIETY

Neoliberalism has not resulted in increased economic growth or greater economic equality but, instead, promotes concentrating power within the corporate and political elite. Moreover, by subordinating ethical and moral considerations to the goal of increasing profits, neoliberalism damages social welfare and the environment. We face the prospect of a future in which all decisions are made on the nexus of profit.

However, neoliberal policies are increasingly resisted at the local, national, and global level. Leitner, Peck & Sheppard (2007) describe how critics are working to

> promote collective rather than individual welfare; collaboration rather than competition; consensual rather than hierarchical decision making; recognition and respect for diversity rather than promotion and commodification of individual identity, equity, justice, and social welfare rather than productivity, growth, and exploitation. (p. 319)

In this final section, I provide examples of how neoliberal policies are being resisted at different political levels and then argue that we need to build a society and schools that will promote democratic deliberative discussions in which we can engage in discussions of not how do we increase profits but what kind of society and world do we want—and then how to work toward those visions.

In Chicago, as Lipman and I describe, teachers' and other school employees' unions, parents' organizations, school reformers, progressive teacher organizations, and advocates for homeless families have formed a loose coalition to oppose Renaissance 2010 and demand that the housing and educational needs of the city's poor and people of color be met. These efforts have gained partial victories, blocked some school closings, and put public school officials and the mayor on the defensive as they are forced to explain and justify the plan. As we note, resistance has led to new alliances across communities and social sectors that had not worked together, bridging racial and ethnic differences and geographic distances, and bringing together unions and communities, professionals and grassroots activists.

In New York City, educators and community members have criticized the mayor and the chancellor's education reforms and have called for the reinstatement of regional boards and an elected school board, and the end of mayoral control (Hancock, 2007). Groups such as Time Out From Testing (www.timeoutfromtesting.org) have lobbied at the local and state levels to repeal high-stakes testing requirements and to reinstate the waiver from Regents tests that were originally granted to the Performance Assessment Schools.

My own efforts have focused not only on research and writing but also on politically pressing for educational and political reforms by working with a group of other educators to establish the Coalition for Common Sense in Education (CCSE) in 1999. Starting in the late 1990s, CCSE (www.commonsense ineducation.org) and Time Out From Testing (TOFT) began campaigning to reinstate the waiver from the Regents exams that had been granted to the twenty-eight schools that make up the Performance Assessment Consortium, which includes the School Without Walls in Rochester and the Urban Academy in New York City (see Cook, 2005). We began by meeting with the commissioner of education and the Board of Regents, who, except for one or two members of the Regents, were deaf to our appeals. We then turned to holding demonstrations in the state capitol and lobbying legislators to reduce the testing requirements. This lobbying contributed to the New York Senate's decision to hold hearings on the exams in fall 2003.

At those hearings, numerous educators who have been involved in the issues of high-stakes testing in New York testified, including Walter Haney (2003), Bill Cala (2003), Dan Drmacich, and Rich Ryan. Bill Cala, as former Fairport Central School District superintendent and interim Rochester City School District superintendent, has actively fought against the Regents and NCLB mandates, including resisting NCLB's requirement that high schools hand over their students' names to the military without explicit parental permission. Dan Drmacich, School Without Walls principal, has led CCSE since the beginning. Richard Ryan, University of Rochester professor, is an internationally renowned researcher on student motivation.

We have also organized numerous community presentations on the current state of education and the effects of high-stakes testing. Speakers have included Jonathan Kozol (2005), Deborah Meier (1995, 2005, & Wood, 2004), Angela Valenzuela (2005), Peter Sacks (1999), and state commissioners of education Douglas Christensen (Nebraska) and Peter McWalters (Rhode Island).

After six years of political organizing, CCSE's efforts paid off with a limited political victory. While the legislature was hesitant to intervene in policy decisions made by the Regents (a system intended to "remove education from politics"), in the summer of 2005, the Republican-controlled state Senate passed a bill that would not only have reinstated the waiver from the Regents requirements granted to the twenty-eight Performance Assessment Consortium Schools but also permitted all school districts to develop alternatives to the standardized Regents exams. The bill then went to the Democratic-controlled Assembly, which, because the Democrats hold a majority of seats in both houses, appoints the members of the Regents and the commissioner. Because the Democrats were not interested in embarrassing those they had appointed and surmised that the Republican governor was likely to veto the bill, members of the Assembly approached the commissioner to reach a compromise: they would not pass the bill if the commissioner would reinstate the waiver. A compromise was reached, and the Consortium Schools were granted a wavier from the social studies and science but not the math and English exams. The waiver was granted up until 2010, at which time the Regents can then reimpose the testing requirements (Herzenhorn, 2005).

However, for CCSE and TOFT, this partial political victory is only the beginning. Reinstating the waiver is necessary but not sufficient. We aim to reduce the impact of the Regents exam so that it is only one of the multiple measures used to assess students (see, e.g., Valenzuela, 2002) and to overhaul, if not repeal, NCLB. Therefore, we continue to wage an educational campaign to reform state and federal education policies, and to meet with political and educational leaders at the state level and, with a new Democratic governor, further reforms look not only possible but also likely.

At the federal level, many education and civil rights groups are working to revise if not repeal the Elementary and Secondary Education Act, the act in which NCLB is embedded. At the outset of the process to reauthorize NCLB, scaling back NCLB seemed unlikely, given that Representative Miller and Senator Kennedy, chairs of their respective education committees, remained "steadfast supporters of the testing and accountability requirements" (Hoff,

2006). My own predictions were not optimistic, given what I have described as the dominance of the neoliberal political vision.

However, resistance from both the political right and left has increased. Some conservative legislators and state governors desire to repeal NCLB because of the federal intrusion on local and state educational policies that were historically determined at the local and state levels (CITE, 2007). Others, such as the Forum on Educational Accountability, an affiliation of 139 civil rights, church, and educational organizations, including the two teachers' unions, are lobbying for significant reforms in NCLB, including using multiple measures and growth models to assess student learning, increasing Title I funding, and funding research and development for more effective accountability systems. (The complete list of their recommended changes can be viewed on their website: http://www.edaccountability.org/Joint_Statement.html)

Furthermore, the public increasingly perceives NCLB as more harmful than good. The August 2007 Phi Delta Kappan/Gallup Poll on the public's attitude toward public schools reveals that the more the public knows about NCLB, the more they are dissatisfied (2007). For example, 40 percent of respondents have a somewhat or very unfavorable view of NCLB, compared to 31 percent who hold the opposite view, and of those who know a great deal or fair amount about NCLB, 55 percent hold a somewhat or very unfavorable view. Fifty-two percent of public school parents, and 43 percent of all respondents, believe testing is overemphasized. Seventy-five percent of parents believe the emphasis on standardized testing encourages teachers to teach toward the test, and 83 percent believe that this is a bad rather than good thing. Moreover, the public is least concerned about standards and quality in schools and most concerned about the lack of funding. All of this points to the possibility of building resistance to the emphasis on testing and efficiency that have become part of the neoliberal efforts.

In critiquing and resisting NCLB, Renaissance 2010, high-stakes testing, and the destruction of public school in New Orleans, it is crucial that these be examined as part of the global effort to impose neoliberal policies on society. Therefore, we need to continually show how the policies are related and also work to repeal neoliberal policies as they affect jobs, housing, health, and our general welfare.

Leitner, Sheppard, Sziarto & Maringanti (2007) describe a broad range of groups contesting neoliberalism at various levels, from the local to the global, and using a variety of strategies. For example, they write that in the United States

> thousands of civic/grassroots organizations are engaged in struggles for living wages, job security, affordable housing, welfare provisions, immigrants' rights, securing equal access to public space, affordable housing, quality public education, alternative modes of transportation, public and environmental health, justice and conservation, seeking to address the need of the "most visibly denuded victims of roll-back neoliberalism" (Peck & Tickell, 2002, p. 393). (p. 18)

Numerous organizations are engaged in combating neoliberalism globally. For example, Walden Bello, the founding director of Focus on the Global South and the author of numerous books, including *The Future in the Balance* (2000) and *Deglobalization: Ideas for a New World Economy* (2004), argues that globalization, "the accelerated integration of capital, production and markets globally; a process driven by corporate profitability," (2004, p. xii) has been combined with "the ideology of neoliberalism, which focused on 'liberating the market' via accelerated privatization, deregulation, and trade liberalization" (p. xiii). His criticisms of neoliberalism include and extend beyond the ones I have offered. He describes how the International Monetary Fund has imposed structural readjustment programs on countries (lower taxes and fewer services) that have "exacerbated stagnation, widened inequalities, and deepened poverty" (p. 5).

In *Deglobalization*, Bello articulates specific economic proposals for "an approach that consciously subordinates the logic of the market, the pursuit of cost efficiency, to the values of security, equity, and social solidarity" (p. 114). His International Forum on Globalization points out that neoliberal policies are economically unsustainable, including, for those in western industrial countries, shipping food thousands of miles (p. 112–113). Indeed, environmental sustainability will require significant rethinking of our economic system and reordering our priorities. The regular gathering of thousands of citizen activists at the World Social Forum in Brazil and regional meetings elsewhere indicate the increasing resistance to neoliberal policies and the argument that another world is possible.

The economist James K. Galbraith (2006) responds to the exportation of jobs to Asia by stating, "if the Indians want call centers and the Chinese want

TV factories, you can't stop them" (p. 199). Instead of policies that only serve to strengthen the market and weaken social welfare, Galbraith calls for "a program of growth and justice," including full employment with meaningful and useful jobs in the United States in essential areas such as teaching and health care, and rebuilding the nation's transportation and energy systems in an "oil-short world." He also calls for "tax fairness, not tax hikes," given our increasingly regressive tax structure in which the poor and the middle class pay more through Social Security, property, and sales taxes, while the rich and corporations pay less.

For the rest of the world, Galbraith argues that a new economic structure should include "egalitarian growth in Europe and Japan, and a worldwide development strategy favoring civil infrastructure and the poor . . . crackdowns on tax havens and the arms trade, a stabilizing financial system and an end to the debt peonage of poor countries" (p. 220).

More centrist politicians, academics, and commentators increasingly recognize the negative consequences free-market neoliberalism has on democracy. For example, Richard Reich, former secretary of labor during the Clinton administration, in *Supercapitalism: The Transformation of Business, Democracy, and Everyday Life* (2007), is alarmed that democracy and equality are in decline as corporations become increasingly able to advance their own interests and ignore the public good.

Moreover, the public is also becoming concerned with the negative consequences of neoliberal policies, especially the way in which the free market harms our health and the environment. Individuals are choosing to opt out of the global food market and to purchase fewer foods transported over a long distance. For example, Barbara Kingsolver, in *Animal, Vegetable, Miracle: A Year of Food Life* (Kingsolver, Kingsolver & Hopp, 2007) and Bill McKibben, in *Deep Economy: The Wealth of Communities and the Durable Future* (2007), describe their efforts to live an environmentally sustainable life.

REASSERTING TEACHING AS A PROFESSION

Education has always been political. Throughout his career, Michael Apple has reminded us that curricular and educational policies reflect particular political ideologies and we, as educators, need to develop alternative pedagogies and policies to disrupt the dominant practices. Luke (2004) cites Apple as lamenting "the failure of progressive and democratic educational constituencies to articulate a forward-looking, strategic alternative to neoliberal governance and teacher de-skilling marks a 'tragic absence' in public debate and educational activism" (p. 1424). Therefore, I want to close by reasserting that educators need to work toward developing an alternative vision for schools and education policy, in particular, and social policy, in general.

Schools can contribute to society by both nurturing and modeling democratic processes and contributing to our knowledge and skills. I described in chapter 3 how students in my school researched and developed a television program, *MAPA Who?*, on urban renewal and suburban sprawl, which was shown on public television and subsequently used by the planning agency to educate the public about planning issues.

In New Orleans, a group of public high school students, who belong to Students at the Center, contributed to the research and writing of the report *Dismantling a Community* (2006), which describes both the process through which, after Hurricane Katrina, the public schools were largely converted into private schools and the students' educational and home experiences before, during, and after the hurricane. The students' eloquent writing about their involvement and commitment to their families, schools, and neighborhood provides glimpses into New Orleans rarely provided by the mainstream media. Students at the Center provides a model for the contribution students can make to our communities.

A more recent example of my own and others' efforts to develop schools in which teachers and students make a difference in the pubic welfare, is the project *Environmental Health Sciences as an Integrative Context for Learning* (see www.niehs.nih.gov/research/supported/programs/ehsic/index.cfm), funded for the last seven years by the National Institute of Environmental Health Sciences, that supported scientists and teacher educators at nine different sites across the United States to work with elementary and secondary teachers in developing and implementing interdisciplinary curricula on the relationship between the environment and human health. While assessing and understanding the risks posed by toxins in our environment requires some scientific knowledge, understanding the danger from and possible remedies for different environmental toxins requires a historical, political, and economic analysis. Furthermore, most of the projects focused on local environmental health problems, such as lead poisoning in Rochester, water pollution in Miami, and poor drinking water in Oregon. At some of the sites, students developed videos, pamphlets, and PowerPoint presentations to educate others, requiring students to develop skills in media technologies, writing, and performing arts. In Rochester, for example, fifth-grade students constructed websites analyzing potential health problems related to pesticides, herbicides, and, their favorite, pet waste; proposed safer alternatives to pesticides and herbicides; and explained how to properly dispose of pet waste. The project had the potential of creating classrooms in which teachers and students contributed to improving the health of their local communities.

Unfortunately, in this case, the historical structure of schools—in which teachers have few opportunities to work across disciplines, the increasing intensification of teachers' work, and the rise of high-stakes testing—made it increasingly impossible to implement the curriculum in schools.

First, teacher collaboration across subject areas has become difficult, if not impossible. Teaching has historically been an isolating profession in which teachers were separated from other teachers. Most schools are designed with classrooms that accommodate one teacher working with a group of students. Classrooms are arranged in an egg carton layout, thus making it possible for teachers to close the classroom door behind them so that they can teach their lessons free from observation. Ruddick (1991) notes, "education is among the last vocations where it is still legitimate to work by yourself in a space that is secure against invaders" (p. 31).

Second, what little time teachers have been given for planning and meeting continues to be reduced through the intensification of teachers' work. This project becomes just one more thing to fit in their school day. In one secondary school, budget cuts have led to increasing the teaching load from five to six periods per day. As one teacher protested, "I would always like *more time*! . . . Time is a real issue" (Martina et al. 2003, p. 7).

Lastly, in addition to the historical constraints of school size and isolation, teachers face the more recent constraint of standardized testing. Because the Environmental Health project is not assessed through any of the various standardized exams, teachers are reluctant to introduce it into any courses in which there is a standardized exam (which, in New York, is almost every secondary course) out of the fear that any time devoted to Environmental Health reduces the amount of time they have to prepare students for the exam. One science teacher stated "the Regents [statewide] exams influence which course it goes into . . . with pressures being what they are to pass these exams and kids having as much trouble as they are passing the upper-level exams, it would be very difficult to do this in a Regents course. . . . The Regents has a prescribed curricula. . . . It makes it very difficult" (Martina, et al., 2003, p. 10). Another teacher added, "High school is more constraining [than in the past] because the stakes are high. Testing is so high. No teacher likes to give up any of their time. You know [teachers do not release students] for band lessons and music lessons" (Martina et al., 2003, p. 11).

While we have been able to introduce Environmental Health into a few local high school classes, those without standardized tests, the other eight sites located around the United States have all but given up on implementing Environmental Health in secondary schools. Instead, they have focused on the elementary and middle school grades in which, until NCLB, fewer standardized tests were given.

However, implementing innovative curriculum in the elementary grades has become difficult. Even before the rise of NCLB's testing requirements, one teacher observed that "standardized testing . . . [is] a problem [for a particular grade] because we . . . teach toward the test . . . [we] spent three weeks cramming for the test." Moreover, because many states' exams and No Child Left Behind focus on math and language arts scores, many states reduced their elementary curriculum to reading, writing, and math. One Texas educator objected, "They are wiping out science for kindergarten through second grade with 'Fundamentals First.' There is no place for anything except reading, writing, arithmetic." And now, with NCLB in full swing, most elementary students face three or more standardized tests per year. One fifth grade teacher in New York, who implemented an environmental health unit in his classroom that culminated in students creating videos, PowerPoint presentations, and websites, no longer teaches the unit because he cannot risk taking time away from preparing students for the four standardized exams spaced throughout the school year.

We need, therefore, teachers to be not only educational leaders in the school but also in the wider community. We need to be aware of how policies such as funding, school design and organization, standardized testing, and NCLB affect our practices and work to develop policies that promote interdisciplinary curriculum, the time and space for teachers to work with one another and community members, and to reflect on one's practice. We need to replace the current high-stakes, "low trust" approach to schooling with approaches that support internal, high-trust accountability based on professional responsibility, "maintained by internal motivations such as commitment, loyalty and sense of duty," with accountability to students, families, communities, and professional peers (Olssen, Codd & O'Neill, 2004, p. 195).

Developing environments in which teachers are delegated professional responsibility, where teachers are trusted, accountable to multiple constituencies, and act deliberatively and morally, requires reorganizing school structures and cultures to promote interdisciplinary teacher collaboration with authentic assessments. The Performance Consortium Schools, which I described earlier, provide a model for redesigning schools as small communities, where all the teachers and students know one another, teachers collaborate in creating curricula and projects based on curricular standards and the students' and teachers' interests, and everyone is held accountable to the community through local boards composed of parents, educators, and community members.

Furthermore, ongoing formative assessments enable teachers and students to evaluate and improve on teaching and learning in ways not possible with summative, high-stakes assessments. As Wood, Darling-Hammond, Neill, and Roscheweski propose in *Refocusing Accountability: Using Local Performance Assessments to Enhance Teaching and Learning for Higher Order Skills* (2007), a briefing paper recently delivered to members of Congress:

> Performance assessments that are locally controlled and involve multiple measures assist students in learning and teachers in teaching for higher order skills. . . . Through using performance assessment, schools can focus instruction on high order skills, provide a more accurate measure of what students know and can do, engage students more deeply in learning, and provide for more timely feedback to teachers, parents, and students in order to monitor and alter discussion. (p. 1)

Performance assessment can also assist in redeveloping trust with the local community. For example, developing the video *MAPA Who?* served as both a culminating project and performance assessment that when shared with parents and the larger community demonstrated the educational accomplishments of the students and the pedagogical expertise of the teachers. Furthermore, sharing performance assessments with the community can form the basis for an ongoing conversation about the educational goals and practices, all of which rebuilds trust in educators.

Moreover, teachers need to work with the wider community to call for more, not less, resources and funding for education, the development of "fully comprehensive schooling" with a "commitment to egalitarian policies aimed at achieving vastly more equal outcomes regardless of factors such as social class, gender, 'race,' sexuality and disability, and the egalitarian redistribution of resources within and between schools, via positive discrimination for underachieving individuals and groups" (Hill, 2007, pp. 215–216).

CONFRONTING THE REAL CRISIS IN EDUCATION

We face a crisis in education different from the one reported in the press. As I have argued throughout, neoliberalism aims to utterly transform the purpose of schooling and society so that economic profit and productivity takes priority over human and environmental welfare. Neoliberals aim to reduce the cost of schooling by increasing efficiency through competitive markets and privatization, and by quantifying progress through standardized tests scores, therefore marginalizing the knowledge and interests of students, teachers, and the community.

Furthermore, the discourse of markets and privatization has become so prevalent that they are difficult to resist. This morning's newspaper brings yet another editorial (Greenhut, 2007) calling for the "complete elimination of the public school system, and its replacement with a true free market. Parents would pay for their own kids' education and would select from a host of private schools that best serve their needs." In response that "the poor" would not be able to afford a private education, Greenhut suggests "that the market (and private charities) will provide an astounding array of excellent choices in the poorest, bleakest neighborhoods." He ends by equating markets to freedom and public schools to communist "central planning" (p. A-8).

One wonders whether Greenhut realizes that an urban school district, even in a midsized city like Rochester, has 36,000 students, of which more than 90 percent live in poverty. How charities would raise the half billion dollars every year necessary to educate all those students is a mystery to me but obviously not to someone who believes that the market solves all problems. Moreover, while Greenhut describes his market solution as providing freedom, it only offers the poor (and most of the middle class) the "freedom" to beg for charity.

The faith that markets and competition should be the basis for decisions is misplaced and misleading. The last two decades of neoliberal dominance has led to increased economic and educational inequality, both nationally and globally. In addition, elevating the economy over all other values, as Bush does when he defends his resistance to policies limiting carbon emissions: "we will not do anything that harms our economy," undermines our ability to make decisions based on values other than profits.

Because neoliberal ideals and processes encompasses almost all of society, including educational goals and processes, reinstating a progressive education focusing on the welfare of people and the planet requires rejecting the neoliberal thesis. We cannot hope that like reforms "this too shall pass." Teachers' historical memories of the possibilities of student and teacher collaborative learning may soon be extinguished and teachers' skills may be reduced to preparing students for multiple-choice exams. Therefore, I urge educators and the public to resist neoliberal education and social policies and develop the schools, social structures, and cultural conditions necessary for an educative society.

What we need, as Anyon (2005) and I (2006) have called for, is a new social movement in which educators work with others to combat not only the rise of high-stakes testing, accountability, markets, and privatization in education, but also the rise of markets and privatization in all of our social policies, and the neoliberal thinking that supports those policies. The real crisis in education is the increasing unwillingness of politicians and the public to realize that markets and privatization are not the solution, but rather the problem. Instead, we need to envision what society should look like if we are to provide everyone with the means to obtain a good education, not only in elementary and secondary school, but also at the university level and beyond. How do we create a society in which everyone has access to health care, a useful and remunerative job, a decent home, and a good education? Moreover, how do we create a society where achieving these goals is an expectation and not left to the vagaries of the market, in which human growth and the health of the planet have precedence over economic growth? As educators, we can take the lead in arguing for policies and practices that counteract the ongoing neoliberal destruction of schools, the environment, and society, and form a society that focuses on examining what we need to know and do to prosper as a people living with the environmental limits of the planet Earth.

References

Adams, M., Blumenfield, W., Casteneda, R., Hackman, H., Peters, M. & Zuniga, X. (2000). Social class questionnaire. In M. Adams (Ed.), *Readings for diversity and social justice: An anthology on racism, sexism, anti-semitism, heterosexism, classism, and ableism* (pp. 432–434). New York: Routledge.

Almaca, J. (2005, September 4). A new catalog: Investments, redevelopment bring buyers to North Lawndale. *Chicago Tribune*, 1-1.

Amrein, A. L. & Berliner, D. C. (2002). High-stakes testing, uncertainty, and student learning. *Education Policy Analysis Archives, 10*(18). Available at: http://epaa.asu .edu/epaa/v10n18/ (accessed April 20, 2005).

Anyon, J. (1997). *Ghetto schooling: A political economy of urban educational reform.* New York: Teachers College Press.

Anyon, J. (2005). *Radical possibilities: Public policy, urban education, and a new social movement.* New York: Routledge.

Apple, M. (1982). *Education and power.* Boston: Routledge and Kegan Paul.

———. (1996). *Cultural politics and education.* New York: Teachers College Press.

———. 2001). *Educating the "right" way: Markets, standards, God, and inequality.* New York: Routledge Falmer.

Arenson, K. (2003, August 27). New York math exam trials showed most students failing. *New York Times*, C-12.

Ayers, W. (2003). *On the side of the child: Summerhill revisited.* New York: Teachers College Press.

Ball, S. J. (1994). *Education reform: A critical and post-structural approach.* Buckingham, UK: Open University Press.

Ball, S. J. (2001). Global policies and vernacular politics in education. *Curriculo sem Fronteiras, 1*(2): xxvii–xliii.

Ball, S. J. (2003). *Class strategies and the education market: The middle classes and social advantage.* London: Routledge Falmer.

Barboza, D. (2007, July 5). China reportedly urged omitting pollution-death estimates. *New York Times,* C-1.

Barlowe, A. & Mack, H. (2002). *Looking for an argument? An inquiry course at Urban Academy Laboratory High School.* New York: Center for Inquiry in Teaching and Learning.

Bauman, Z. (1999). *In search of politics.* Stanford, CA: Stanford University Press.

Bauman, Z. (2000). *Liquid modernity.* Cambridge, UK: Polity Press.

Becker, G. (1976). *The economic approach to human behavior.* Chicago: University of Chicago Press.

Bello, W. (2004). *Deglobalization: Ideas for a new world economy.* New York: Zed Books.

Bello. W. (2005). *Dilemmas of domination: The unmaking of the American empire.* New York: Metropolitan Books.

Bennett, L. (1998). Do we really live in a communtarian city?: Communitarian thinking and the redevelopment of Chicago's Cabrini-Gren public housing complex. *Journal of Urban Affairs, 20*(2): 99–116.

Bennett, L. (2002). Do we really wish to live in a communitarian city? Communitarian thinking and the redevelopment of Chicago's Cabrini-Green public housing complex. *Journal of Urban Affairs, 20*(2): 99–116.

Bennett, M. (2007). The rebirth of Bronzeville: Community renewal or poor folk removal? In J. P. Koval, L. Bennet & F. Demisse (Eds.), *The new Chicago: A social and cultural analysis.* Philadelphia: Temple University Press.

Berger, J. (2007, June 13). This is a test. Results may vary. *New York Times,* B-1.

Berliner, D. & Biddle. B. (1995). *The manufactured crisis: Myths, fraud and the attack on America's public schools.* Reading, MA: Addison Wesley.

Bluestein, B. (2005). A new business plan for Chicago. Executive Agenda, first quarter, 2005. A. T. Kearney. Available at: www.atkearney.com/main .taf?p=5,1,1,110,6 (accessed April 12, 2005).

Bobbitt, F. (1912, February). The elimination of waste in education. *Elementary School Teacher*, 12: 259–271.

Bobbitt, F. (1918). *The curriculum*. New York: Houghton Mifflin.

Bobbitt. F. (1924). *How to make a curriculum*. New York: Houghton Mifflin.

Bonilla-Silva, E. (2001). *White supremacy and racism in the post-civil rights era*. Boulder, CO: Lynne Rienner Publishers.

Borja, R. (2006, December 20). Market for NCLB tutoring falls short of expectations. *Education Week, 26*(16): 5, 13.

Bosman, J. (2007, June 9). A plan to pay for top scores on some tests gains ground. *New York Times*, B-1.

Bourdieu, P. (1986). The forms of capital. In J. G. Richardson (Ed.), *Handbook of theory and research for the sociology of education* (pp. 241–258). New York: Greenwood.

Bourdieu, P. (1998). *Act of resistance: Against the tyranny of the market*. New York: The New Press.

Bourdieu, P. & Passeron, J. C. (1977). *Reproduction in education, society, and culture*. Berkeley and Los Angeles: University of California Press.

Bowles, S. & Gintis, H. (1986). *Democracy and capitalism: Property, community and the contradictions of modern thought*. New York: Basic Books.

Bracey, G. (2004, October). The 14th Bracey report on the condition of public education. *Phi Delta Kappan*, 149–167.

Bracey, G. (2006, October). The 16th Bracey report on the condition of public education. *Phi Delta Kappan*, 151–166.

Bracey, G. (2007). The rotten apple awards in education for 2006. Available at: http://www.america-tomorrow.com/bracey/EDDRA/

Bradsher, K. (2003, October 22). China's boom adds to global warming. *New York Times*, A-1, A-8.

Brenner, N. & Theodore, N. (2002). Cities and the geographies of "actually existing neoliberalism." In N. Brenner & N. Theodore (Eds.), *Spaces of neoliberalism:*

Urban restructuring in North American and Western Europe (pp. 2–32). Oxford, UK: Blackwell.

Brodkin, K. (2001). How Jews became white. In P. Rothenburg (Ed.), *Race, class, and gender in the United States* (pp. 30–46). New York: Worth.

Byrk, A. S. (2003). No Child Left Behind, Chicago style, in P. W. Peterson & M. West (Eds.), *No Child Left Behind? The politics and practice of school accountability* (pp. 242–268). Washington, DC: Brookings Institute Press.

Bryk, A. S., Sebring, P. B., Kerbow, D., Rollow, S., & Easton, J. Q. (1998). *Charting Chicago school reform: Democratic localism as a lever for change.* Boulder: Westview Press.

Buchanan, J. (1975). *The limits of liberty: Between anarchy and leviathan.* Chicago: University of Chicago Press.

Cala, W. (2003, October 22). Testimony before the New York Senate Standing Committee on Education, Roosevelt Hearing Room C, Legislative Office Building, Albany, New York. Available at: http://www.timeoutfromtesting.org/testimonies.php (accessed September 15, 2005).

Cala, W. (2004). The mismeasure and abuse of our children: Why school officials must resist state and national testing reforms. In S. Mathison & E. W. Ross (Eds.), *Defending public schools: The nature and limits of standards-based reform and assessment.* vol. 4 (pp. 149–165). Westport, CT: Praeger.

Cazden, C. B. (1988). Classroom discourse: The language of teaching and learning. Portsmouth, NH: Heinemann.

Capellaro, C. (2004). Blowing the whistle on the Texas miracle: An interview with Robert Kimball. *Rethinking Schools* 19(1). Available at: http://www.rethinkingschools.org (accessed October 1, 2004).

Carr, W. & Kemmis, S. (1986). *Becoming critical: Education, knowledge and action research.* London: Falmer.

Center for Community Change (2006, September). *Dismantling a community.* Washington, DC: Center for Community Change. Available at: http://www.cccfiles.org/issues/education/publications (accessed December 2, 2007).

Chicago Housing Authority (CHA) (2000). *CHA Plan for Transformation.* Available at: www.thecha.org (accessed June 1, 2005).

Chicago Public Schools (CPS) Policy Manual (2004, September 22). Establish Renaissance schools. Sec. 302.7. Available at: http://policy.cps.k12.il.us/ documents/302.7.pdf (accessed September 25, 2004).

Chicago Public Schools (2004, June 8). Press release. Daley announces Renaissance 2010. Available at: www.cps.k12.il.us/AboutCPS/Press Releases/June_2004/ Renaissance2010.html (accessed July 8, 2004).

Chicago Public Schools (2004, September 9). Press release. Community leaders join Duncan at new West Side HS to support Renaissance 2010. Available at: www.cps.k12.il.us/AboutCPS/PressReleases/September_2004/2010_community_v oice.htm (accessed September 25, 2004).

Chicago Public Schools (2004, September 22). Press release. Chicago Board of Education approves policy for opening new schools under Renaissance 2010. Available at: www.cps.k12.il.us/AboutCPS/PressReleases/September_2004/ 2010_policy_approval.htm. (accessed September 25, 2004).

Chicago Metropolis 2020 (2001). *Regional realities.* Chicago: Chicago Metropolis 2020.

Chicago Metropolis 2020 (2002). *The metropolis index, 2002.* Chicago: The Commercial Club of Chicago.

Cholo, A. B. (2005, February 23). Businesses help new schools. *Chicago Tribune Online Edition,* (accessed February 24, 2005).

Cholo, A. B. & Little, D. (2003, August 10). Some schools left behind by fine print. *Chicago Tribune,* 4-1, 6.

Chubb, J. E. & Moe, T. M. (1990). *Politics, markets, and America's schools.* Washington, DC: Brookings Institution.

Civic Committee of the Commercial Club of Chicago (2003). *Left Behind.* A report of the Education Committee of the Civic Committee. Chicago: Commercial Club of Chicago.

Civic Committee of the Commercial Club of Chicago (2004, June 24). Press release. Chicago business leaders applaud Renaissance 2010—pledge financial and technical support. Available at: http://www.lqe.org/News%20&%20Events/ 100NEWSchools-PressRelease.pdf (accessed September 26, 2005).

Clarke, J. (2007). Citizen consumers and public service reform: At the limits of neoliberalism? *Policy Futures in Education* 5(2): 239–248.

Coalition to Protect Public Housing (CPPH) (2005, June 23). Press release. CHA plan for Cabrini-Green still not complete. Available at: http://www.limits.com/cpph/ (accessed November 25, 2005).

Cook, A. (2005, Summer). Standardizing small. *Rethinking Schools, 19*(4): 15–17.

Counts, G. (1932). *Dare the school build a new social order?* New York: John Day.

CPS School Board Meeting. (2004, August 25 and September 22). Field Notes.

Dale, R. (1989/1990). The Thatcherite project in education: The case of the City Technology Colleges. *Critical Social Policy,* 9: 4–19.

Dale, R. & Robertson, S. (2004). Interview with Boaventura de Sousa Santo. *Globalization, Societies and Education,* 2(2): 147–160.

Darling-Hammond, L. (2006, October). Securing the right to learn: Policy and practices for powerful teaching and learning. *Educational Researcher, 35*(7): 13–24.

Dean, M. (2002). Liberal government and authoritarianism. *Economy and Society, 31*(1): 37–61.

DeBray, E. (2006). *Politics, ideology, and education: Federal policy during the Clinton and Bush administrations.* New York: Teachers College Press.

Dennison, G. (1969). *The lives of children: The story of the First Street School.* New York: Random House.

Dewey, J. (1894, August 25–26). John Dewey to Alice Chipman Dewey and children. Letter. *John Dewey Papers.* Special Collections, Morris Library, Southern Illinois University.

Dewey, J. (1915a). *The child and the curriculum and the school and society.* Chicago: University of Chicago Press.

Dewey, J. (1915b, May 5). Untitled. *The New Republic 3:* 42.

Dewey, J. (1950). *Reconstruction in philosophy.* New York: The New American Library.

Dewey, J. (1963). *Education and experience.* New York: Macmillian/Collier (originally published in 1938).

Dewey, J. (1987). Democracy and educational admnistration, in J. A. Boydson (Ed.), *John Dewey: The later works,* 1925–1953. Carbondale and Edwardsville, IL: Southern Illinois University.

Dingerson, L. (2006, Fall). Dismantling a community: In Katrina's wake, a baffling array of school systems has been created. *Rethinking Schools,* 21(1): 7–13.

Drost, W. H. (1967). *David Snedden and education for social efficiency.* Madison: University of Wisconsin Press.

Eberling, R. M. (2000, February). *It's time to put public education behind us.* Future of Freedom Foundation Commentaries. Available at: http://www.fff.org/comment/ed0200f.asp.

Editors. (2006, Fall). Educational land grab. *Rethinking Schools* 21(1): 5–6.

Education Review (2003, September 26). *International Report.* U.S. Office of Education listserve. Available at: http://www.ed.gov/news/newsletter/edreview/20030926.html (accessed October 3, 2003).

Fairclough, N. (2003). *Analyzing discourse: Textual analysis for social research.* New York: Routledge.

Fairclough, N. (2006). *Language and globalization.* New York: Routledge.

Faux, J. (2006). *The global class war: How America's bipartisan elite lost our future— and what it will take to win it back.* New York: Wiley.

Field, J. (2005, May 5). Renaissance 2010 off-track? Chicago Public Radio, *Eight Forty-Eight.*

Fine, M. (2005, Summer). Not in our name. *Rethinking Schools* 19(4): 11–14.

Fine, M., Torre, M. E., Boudin, K., Bowen, I, Clark, J., & Hylton, D. (2005). Participatory action research: From within and beyond prison bars. In L. Weis & M. Fine (Eds.), *Working method: Research and social justice* (pp. 95–110). New York: Routledge.

Finkel, E. (2005, May 5). Renaissance 2010 off track? Chicago Public Radio *Eight Forty-Eight.*

Fischer, H. (1999, December 8). Bush places free trade above land, labor issues. *Arizona Daily Star,* 15-A.

Fones-Wolfe, E. (1994). *Selling free-enterprise: The business assault on labor and liberalism 1945–1960.* Urbana: University of Illinois Press.

Foucault, M. (1979, March 14). "The birth of bio-politics": Michel Foucault's lecture at the College de France on neo-liberal governmentality. *Economy and Society,* 30(2): 198.

Friedman, B. (2002, August 15). Globalization: Stiglitz's case. *New York Review of Books.*

Friedman, M. (1952). *Essays on positive economics.* Chicago: University of Chicago Press.

Friedman, M. (1962). *Capitalism and freedom.* Chicago: University of Chicago Press.

Friedman, M. (1995, June 23). Public Schools: Make them private. Cato Briefing paper No. 23. Available at: http:www.cato.org/pubs/briefs/bp-023.html (accessed November 26, 2007).

Friedman, T. (1999). *The Lexus and the olive tree.* New York: Farrar, Straus & Giroux.

Friedman, T. L. (2005). *The world is flat: A brief history of the twenty-first century.* New York: Farrar, Straus & Giroux.

Fulbright, J. W. (1966). *The arrogance of power.* New York: Random House.

Fung, A. (2004). *Empowered participation: Reinventing urban democracy.* Princeton: Princeton University Press.

Galbraith, J. K. (2006). *Unbearable cost: Bush, Greenspan and the economics of empire.* New York: Palgrave Macmillan.

Gandin, L. (2007). The construction of the Citizen School Project as an alternative to neoliberal educational policies. *Policy Futures in Education* 5(2): 179–193.

Gandin, L. A. & Apple, M. W. (2003). Educating the state, democratizing knowledge: The Citizen School Project in Porto Alegre, Brazil. In M. W. Apple, *The state and the politics of knowledge* (pp. 193–219). New York: Routledge.

Gilbert, R. & Gilbert, P. (1998). *Masculinity goes to school.* New York: Routledge.

Gill, S. (2003). *Power and resistance in the new world order.* New York: Palgrave Macmillan.

Gillborn, D. & Youdell, D. (2000). *Rationing education: Policy, practice, reform and equity.* Philadelphia, PA: Open University Press.

Goldberg, J. (2007, June 5). Public schools flunk every course. *Democrat and Chronicle,* A-12.

Goodman, P. (1960). *Growing up absurd: Problems of youth in the organized system.* New York: Random House.

Goodman, P. (1962). *Utopian essays and practical proposals.* New York: Random House.

Goodman, P. (1964). *Compulsory miseducation.* New York: Horizon.

Gotbaum, B. (2002). *Pushing out at-risk students: An analysis of high school discharge figures.* New York: Public School Advocate for the City of New York and Advocates for Children.

Gould, S. J. (1981). *The mismeasure of man.* New York: W.W. Norton.

Graubard, A. (1972). *Free the children: Radical school reform and the free school movement.* New York: Pantheon.

Greene, M. (1967). (Ed.) *Existential encounters for teachers.* New York: Random House.

Greene, M. (1978). *Landscapes of learning.* New York: Teachers College Press.

Greene, M. (1988). *Dialectic of freedom.* New York: Teachers College Press.

Greene, M. (1995). *Releasing the imagination.* San Francisco: Jossey-Bass.

Greene, M. (1998). Towards beginning. In W. Pinar (Ed.), *The passionate mind of Maxine Greene: "I am . . . not yet"* (pp. 256–257). Bristol, PA: Falmer Press.

Greenhut, S. (2007, June 21). Eliminate public school systems. *Democrat and Chronicle,* A-8.

Grossman, R. & Leroux, C. (2006, January 29). The unmaking of a ghetto. *Chicago Tribune Magazine,* 11–16, 26–29.

Gutmann, A. & Thompson, D. (2004). *Why deliberative democracy?* Princeton, NJ: Princeton University Press.

Haar, C. K. (1996, September/October). Special interests in the classroom: Fixing America's schools. *American Enterprise Online.* Available at: http://www.taemag .com/issues/articleID.16288/article_detail.asp (accessed March 16, 2004).

Hacker, A. (1993). *Two nations: Black and white, separate, hostile.* New York: Ballantine Books.

Hakim, D. & Arenson, K. (2007, May 30). Spitzer names a panel to improve universities in New York. *New York Times,* B-8.

Hall, S. (1998). The great moving nowhere show. *Marxism Today,* 9–14.

Hancock, L. (2007, July 9). School's out. *The Nation,* 16–17, 20–21.

Handley, J. (2004, August 22). Redeveloping public housing. *Chicago Tribune,* C-1.

Haney, W. (2000, August 19). The myth of the Texas Miracle in education. *Education Policy Analysis Archives*. Available at: http://epaa.asu.edu/epaa/v8n41 (accessed May 15, 2005).

Haney, W. (2003, September 23). *Attrition of students from New York Schools*. Invited testimony at public hearing, New York Senate, Standing Committee on Education, *Regents Learning Standards and High School Graduation Requirements*. Available at: http://www.timeoutfromtesting.org/testimonies/923_Testimony_Haney.pdf (accessed October 5, 2003).

Hansen, J. (2006, January 12). The tipping point (from a presentation to the American Geophysical Association, December 6, 2005). *New York Review of Books*, 53(1): 19.

Harvey, D. (2001). *Spaces of capital: Towards a critical geography*. London: Routledge.

Harvey, D. (2005). *A brief history of neoliberalism*. Oxford, UK: Oxford University.

Hatcher, R. (2003, December 12). Business agenda and school education in England. Available at: http://www. Socialist-teacher.org/dossiers.asp?d=y&id=75 (accessed December 11, 2007).

Hayden, C. (2001, May 7). Letter to the Hon. Richard Brodsky and Hon. Richard Green, NY State Assembly.[AQ7]

Hayek, F. A. (1944). *The road to serfdom*. Chicago: University of Chicago Press.

Hayek, F. A. (1960). *The constitution of liberty*. Chicago: Henry Regnery.

Haymes, S. N. (1995). *Race, culture and the city*. Albany: State University of New York Press.

Henwood, D. (2003). *After the new economy*. New York: The New Press.

Heritage Foundation. (2005, September 7). *From tragedy to triumph: Principled solutions for rebuilding lives and communities*. Webmemo #83. Available at: www.heritage.org/Research/GovernmentReform/wm835.cfm (accessed December 2, 2007).

Herszenhorn, D. (2005, June 22). State Agrees for 28 Schools to Stay Free of Regents Tests. *New York Times*.

Hill, D. (2007). Critical teacher education, new labor, and the global project of neoliberal capital. *Policy Futures in Education*, 5(2): 204–225.

Hobbes, T. (1968). *Leviathan*, ed. C. B. Macpherson. London: Penguin.

Hoff, D. (2006, November 15). Democratic majority to put education policy on agenda. *Education Week*, 26(12): 1, 26–27.

Holt, J. (1964). *How children fail*. New York: Pitman.

Holt, J. (1969). *How children learn*. New York: Pitman.

Hursh, D. (1979, January 10). A child-centered language-arts curriculum. *Flint*, p. 6.

Hursh. D. (2003). Discourse, power, and resistance in New York: The rise of testing and accountability and the decline of teacher professionalism and local control. In J. Satterthwaite, J, Atkinson & K. Gale (Eds.), *Discourse, power, resistance: Challenging the rhetoric of contemporary education*, (pp. 43–56). Stoke-on-Trent, UK: Trentham.

Hursh, D. (2004). Undermining democratic education in the U.S.: The consequences of global capitalism and neo-liberal policies for education policies at the local, state, and federal levels. *Policy Futures in Education* 2(3/4): 601–614.

Hursh, D. (2005a). Neoliberalism, markets and accountability: Transforming education and undermining democracy in the United Stated and England. *Policy Futures in Education* 3(1): 3–15.

Hursh, D. (2005b, October). The growth of high-stakes testing, accountability and education markets and the decline of educational equality. *British Educational Research Journal* 31(5): 605–622.

Hursh, D. (2006, May). The crisis in urban education: Resisting neoliberal policies and forging democratic possibilities. *Educational Researcher* 35(4): 19–25.

Hursh, D. (2007a). Introduction. *Policy Futures in Education: Theme Issue on Neoliberalism* 5(2): 115–118.

Hursh, D. (2007b). Neoliberalism. In D. Gabbard (Ed.), *Knowledge and power in the global economy: The effects of school reform in a neoliberal/neoconservative age*. Mahwah, NJ: Lawrence Erlbaum.

Hursh, D. & Martina, C. A. (October 2003). Neoliberalism and schooling in the U.S.: How state and federal government education policies perpetuate inequality. *Journal of Critical Education Policy Studies*. vol. 1 and 2. Available at: http://www.jceps.com/?pageID=article&articleID=12 (accessed December 11, 2007).

Hursh D. & Ross E. W. (Eds.) (2000). *Democratic social education: Social studies for social change*. London: Falmer.

Hursh, D. & Seneway, A. (1998). Living, not practicing democracy. *Theory and Research in Social Education 26*(2): 258–262.

Hursh, D. & Seneway, A. (2001). Standards, not standardization: Learning in a democratic classroom. In J. Kincheloe & D. Weil (Eds.), *The Encyclopedia of Educational Standards* (pp. 313–323). Santa Barbara, CA: ABC-Clio.

Johnson, D. C. & Salle, L. M. (2004, November). *Responding to the attack on public education and teacher unions: A Commonweal Institute report.* Menlo Park, CA: Commonweal Institute. Available at: http://www.commonwealinstitute.org/IssuesEducation.htm (accessed November 25, 2004).

Johnson, E. (1998, November). Executive summary. In *Chicago Metropolis 2020: Preparing Metropolitan Chicago for the 21st Century.* Chicago: Commercial Club of Chicago.

Jomo, K. S. & Baudot, J. (2007). Preface. In K. S. Jomo and J. Baudot (Eds.), *Flat world, big gaps: Economic liberalization, globalization, poverty, and inequality* (pp. xvii–xxvii). New York: Zed Books.

Kanigel, R. (2005). *The one best way: Frederick Winslow Taylor and the enigma of efficiency (Sloan technology).* Cambridge, MA: MIT Press.

Katz, M. B. (1992). Chicago school reform as history. *Teachers College Record, 94*(1): 56–72.

Katz, M., Fine, M., & Simon, E. (1997). Poking around: Outsiders view Chicago school reform. *Teachers College Record 99*(1): 117–157.

Katznelson, I. (2005). *When affirmative action was white: An untold history of racial inequality in twentieth-century America.* New York: W.W. Norton.

Kearney, A. T. (2004). *A team of knowledgeable people who produce extraordinary results.* A. T. Kearney website homepage. Available at: http://www.atkearney.com/main.taf?p=1 (accessed October 7, 2004).

Kearney, A. T. (2005). *A new business plan for Chicago Public Schools.* Available at: http://www.atkearney.com/main.taf?p=5,1,1,114,6,1 (accessed May 6, 2005).

Kincheloe, J. L. (2001). Hope in the shadows: Reconstructing the debate over educational standards. In J. L. Kincheloe & D. Weil (Eds.), *Standards and schooling in the United States: An encyclopedia.* vol. 1 (pp. 1–104). Santa Barbara, CA: ABC-Clio.

Kingsolver, B., Kingsolver, C., & Hopp, S. (2007). *Animal, vegetable, miracle: A year of food life.* New York: HarperCollins.

Kliebard, H. (1999). *Schooled to work: Vocationalism and the American curriculum, 1876–1946.* New York: Teachers College Press.

Kliebard, H. (1986). *The struggle for the American curriculum: 1893–1958.* 3rd ed. New York: Routledge.

Klein, A. (2007, February 14). Bush budget would boost NCLB efforts. *Education Week 26*(23): 1, 25.

Klein, N. (2007). *The shock doctrine: The rise of disaster capitalism.* New York: Henry Holt and Company.

Kleinfield, N. (2002, June 6). The elderly man and the sea? Test sanitizes literacy texts. *New York Times,* A-1.

Kohl, H. (1967). *36 children.* New York: New American Library.

Kohl, H. (1969). *The open classroom: A practical guide to a new way of teaching.* New York: New York Review.

Kohl, H. (1976). *On teaching.* New York: Schocken Books.

Kozol, J. (1967). *Death at an early age: The destruction of the hearts and minds of Negro children in the Boston Public Schools.* Boston: Houghton Mifflin.

Kozol, J. (1972). *Free schools.* Boston: Houghton Mifflin.

Kozol, J. (1991). *Savage inequalities: Children in America's schools.* New York: Crown.

Kozol. J. (2005). *The shame of the nation: The restoration of apartheid schooling in America.* New York: Crown Publishing.

Lague, D. (2005, November 24). Water crisis shows China's pollution risk. *New York Times,* A-4.

Lauder, H., Brown, P., Dillabough, J.-A., & Halsey, A. H. (2006). Introduction. The prospects for education: Individualization, globalization, and social change. In H. Lauder, P. Brown, J.-A. Dillabough & A. H. Halsey (Eds.), *Education, globalization and social change* (pp. 1–70). Oxford, UK: Oxford University Press.

Lee, J. (2006, June). *Tracking achievement gaps and assessing the impact of NCLB on the gaps: An in-depth look into national and state reading and math outcome trends.* Cambridge, MA: The Civil Rights Project of Harvard University.

Leitner, H., Sheppard, E. S., & Peck, J. (Eds.) (2007). *Contesting neoliberalism: Urban frontiers.* New York: Guilford Press.

Leitner, H., Sheppard, E. S., Sziarto, K., & Maringanti, A. (2007). Contesting urban futures: Decentering neoliberalism. In H. Leitner, E. S. Sheppard & J. Peck (Eds.), *Contesting neoliberalism: Urban frontiers* (pp. 1–25). New York: Guilford Press.

Lemert, C. (1997). *Social things: An introduction to the sociological life.* Lanham, MD: Rowman & Littlefield.

Lemke, T. (2001). "The birth of bio-politics": Michel Foucault's lecture at the College de France on neo-liberal governmentality, *Economy and Society, 30*(2): 190–207.

Lemke, T. (2002, Fall). Foucault, governmentality and critique. *Rethinking Marxism,* 14(3): 49–64.

Levitas, R. (Ed.) (1986). *The ideology of the New Right.* Cambridge, UK: Polity Press.

Linn, R. (2003). Accountability: Responsibility and reasonable expectations. *Educational Researcher, 32*(7): 3–13.

Lipman, P. (2002). Making the global city, making inequality: The political economy and cultural politics of Chicago school policy. *American Educational Research Journal, 39*(2): 379–419.

Lipman, P. (2003). Chicago school policy: Regulating black and Latino youth in the global city. *Race, Ethnicity and Education, 6*(4): 331–355.

Lipman, P. (2004). *High stakes education: Inequality, globalization, and urban school reform.* New York: Routledge.

Lipman, P. (2005). We're not blind. Just follow the dollar sign. *Rethinking Schools,* 19(4): 54–58.

Lipman, P. & Gutstein, E. (2001). Undermining the struggle for equity: A case study of Chicago school policy in a Latino/a school. *Race, Gender and Class, 8*(1): 57–80.

Lipman, P. & Haines, N. (2007). From education accountability to privatization and African American exclusion—the case of Chicago Public Schools. *Educational Policy 21*(3): 471–502.

Lipman P. & Hursh, D. (2007). Renaissance 2010: The reassertion of ruling class power through neoliberal policies in Chicago. *Policy Futures in Education, 5*(2): 160–178.

Little, J. W. & McLaughlin, M. W. (1993). *Teachers' work: Individuals, colleagues, and contexts.* New York: Teachers College Press.

Locke, J. (1690/1960). *Two treatises on government.* P. Laslett (Ed.) Cambridge: Cambridge University Press.

Luke, A. (2004). Teaching after the market: From commodity to cosmopolitan. *Teachers College Record, 106*(7): 1422–1443.

Markley, M. (2004, April 1). TAAS scores rose as SATs fell. *Houston Chronicle,* A-1.

Martina, C., Hursh, D., Markowitz,. D., Hart, K., & Debes, P. (2003, October). Contradictions in Educational Policy: Developing Integrated Problem-based Curriculum in a High-stakes Environment. American Educational Studies Association Conference, Mexico City, Mexico.

Marx, K. (1932). *The German ideology.* Moscow: Marx-Engels Institute.

Matthews, C. (2007, October, 24). Senate OKs Spitzer appointees. *Poughkeepsie Journal* Available at: http://www.poughkeepsie journal.com/apps/pbcs.dll/article?AID=/20071024/NEW01/710240304/1006/NEWS (accessed November 28, 2007).

McDermott, M. (2007, February 7). Greece hosts "World is flat" talk. *Democrat and Chronicle,* B-3.

McKibben, B. (2006, January 12). The coming meltdown. *New York Review of Books, 53*(1), 16–18.

McKibben, B. (2007). *Deep economy: The wealth of communities and the durable future.* New York: Times Books.

McLaren, P. & Jaramillo, N. (2007). *Pedagogy and praxis in the age of empire: Towards a new humanism.* Rotterdam: Sense Publications.

McNeil, L. (2000). *Contradictions of school reform: Educational costs of standardized testing.* New York: Routledge.

McNeil, L. & Valenzuela, A. (2001). The harmful impact of the TAAS system of testing on Texas: Beneath the accountability rhetoric. In G. Orfield & M. L. Kornhaber (Eds.), *Raising standards or raising barriers? Inequality and high stakes testing in public education* (pp. 127–150). New York: Century Foundation Press.

Meier, D. (1995). *The power of their ideas: Lessons for America from a small urban high school.* Boston: Beacon.

Menand, L. (2001). *The metaphysical club: A story of ideas in America.* New York: Farrar, Straus & Giroux.

Michaels Development Corporation. (2003). Legends South Formerly Known as Robert Taylor Homes. Available at: www.michaelsdevelopment company.com/portfRobertTaylor.html (accessed December 2, 2005).

Midsouth: Education Plan Renaissance 2010 Fact Sheet (n.d.). Kenwood Oakland Local School Council Alliance. Chicago. Available at: www.teachersforjustice .org/pages/R2010factsheet.html. (accessed December 2, 2007).

Mills, C. W. (1959). *The sociological imagination.* Oxford: Oxford University Press.

Minding the gap: An assessment of racial disparity in metropolitan Chicago. (2003). Chicago: Hull House Association.

Miner, B. (2004, Summer). Seed money for conservatives. *Rethinking Schools, 18*(4): 9–11.

Monk, D., Sipple, J., & Killeen, K. (2001, September 10). Adoption and adaptation, New York State school districts' responses to state imposed high school graduation requirements: An eight-year retrospective. *Education Finance Research Consortium.* Available at: www.albany.edu/edfin/CR01_MSk_Report.pdf (accessed March 3, 2002).

National Center on Education and the Economy (2007). *Tough choices or tough times: The report on the new commission on the skills of the American workforce.* San Francisco: Jossey-Bass.

National Commission on Excellence in Education (NCEE) (1983). *A nation at risk: A report to the nation and the Secretary of Education.* Washington, DC: U.S. Department of Education.

National Defense Education Act (1958). Public Law 85-864, 85th Congress, September 2, 1958.

National Research Council (1999). *How people learn: Bridging research and practice.* Committee on Learning Research and Educational Practice. M. S. Donovan, J. D. Bransford & J. W. Pelligrino (Eds.), Commission on Behavioral and Social Sciences and Education. Washington, DC: National Academies Press.

National Research Council (2001). *Knowing what students know: The science and design of educational assessment.* J. W. Pelligrino, N. Chudowsky & R. Glaser (Eds.) Committee on the Foundations of Assessment. Washington, DC: National Academies Press.

Neil, A. S. (1960). *Summerhill: A radical approach to child rearing.* New York: Hart Publishing Company.

Newman, D., Griffin, P., & Cole, M. (1989). *The construction zone: Working for cognitive change in school.* Cambridge, MA: Cambridge University Press.

New York State School Boards Association (NYSSBA) (2002, September 16). Title I accountability status updated for March 10, 2003. Available at: http://www.nyssba .org/adnews/misc/thenewaccountability-5.htm (accessed August 28, 2003).

Newmann, F. M., Bryk, A. S., & Nagaoka, J. K. (2001, January). *Authentic intellectual work and standardized test: Conflict or coexistence?* A report of the Chicago Annenberg Research Project. Chicago: Consortium on Chicago School Research.

No Child Left Behind Act of 2001 (2001). 20 U.S.C. § 603.

Nozick, R. (1974). *Anarchy, state and utopia.* Oxford, UK: Blackwell.

Olssen, M., Codd, J., & O'Neill, A. M. (2004). *Education policy: Globalization, citizenship and democracy.* Thousand Oaks, CA: Sage.

Orfield, G. (1990). Wasted talent, threatened future: Metropolitan Chicago's human capital and Illinois public policy. In L. B. Joseph (Ed.), *Creating jobs, creating workers: Economic development and employment in metropolitan Chicago* (pp. 129–160). Chicago: University of Chicago Center for Urban Research and Policy Studies.

Orfield, G. (2006). Forward. *Tracking achievement gaps and assessing the impact of NCLB on the gaps: An in-depth look into national and state reading and math outcome trends.* Cambridge, MA: The Civil Rights Project of Harvard University.

Orfield, G. & Eaton, S. (1996). *Dismantling desegregation: The quiet reversal of Brown v. Board of Education.* New York: New Press.

Orfield, G., Losen, D., Wald, J., & Swanson, C. (2004). *Losing our future: How minority youth are being left behind by the graduation rate crisis.* Cambridge, MA: The Civil Rights Project at Harvard University.

Paige, R. & Jackson, A. (2004, November 8). Education: The civil-rights issue of the twenty-first century. *Hispanic Vista.* Available at: http://hispanicvista.com/HVC/ Opinion/Guest-Columns/1108Rod_Paige-Alponso_Jackson.htm. (accessed December 11, 2007).

Paley, A. R. (2007, June 26). Ex-aides break with Bush on "No Child": Conservatives giving vent to doubts: support for opt-out proposals grows. *Washington Post,* p. A04

Paley, A. (2007, January 25). Bush proposes adding private school vouchers to "No Child" law. *Washington Post,* A-16.

Parenti, C. (1999). Atlas finally shrugged: Us against them in the me decade. *The Baffler,* 13: 108–120.

Pedroni, T. C. (2007). *Market movements: African American involvement in school voucher reform.* New York: Routledge.

Peters, M. (1994, June). Individualism and community: Education and the politics of difference. *Discourse: Studies in the Cultural Politics of Education, 14*(2): 65–78.

Petrovich, J. & Wells, A. S. (Eds.) (2005). *Bringing equity back: Research for a new era in American educational policy.* New York: Teachers College Press.

Polyani, K. (1954). *The great transformation.* Boston: Beacon Press.

Popkin, S. J., Cunningham, M. K., & Woodley, W. (2003). *Residents at risk.* Urban Institute. Available at: http://www.urban.org/url.cfm?ID=310824 (accessed March 25, 2004).

Postman, N. & Weingartner, C. (1969). *Teaching as a subversive activity.* New York: Delacorte Press.

Reed, A. (2006, September 18). Undone by neoliberalism. *The Nation, 283*(8): 26–30.

Reich, R. (2007). *Supercapitalism: The transformation of business, democracy, and everyday life.* New York: Knopf.

Rethinking Schools (2005). Special issue: Is small beautiful? The promise and problems of small school reform. 19(4).

Rich, A. (1993). *What is found there: Notebooks on poetry and politics.* New York: W.W. Norton.

Rich, A. (2001). Arts of the possible. In A. Rich (Ed.), *Arts of the possible.* New York: W.W. Norton.

Rivera, M. (2003, June 19). Personal communication from the superintendent of Rochester (NY) City Schools.

Rivlin, G. (1992). *Fire on the prairie: Chicago's Harold Washington and the politics of race.* New York: Henry Holt and Company.

Robertson, S. (2000). *A class act: Changing teachers' work, the state, and globalization.* Philadelphia: Falmer Press.

Robertson, S. (2003). The politics of re-territorialization: Space, scale and teachers as a professional class. In H. Athanasaides & A. Patramanis (Eds.), *Teachers and European integration* (pp. 41–69). Athens: Educational Institute.

Robertson, S. & Dale, R. (2003) Changing geographies of power in education: The politics of rescaling and its contradictions. Chapter presented to the Joint

BERA/BAICE Conference on Globalization, Culture and Education, June 12, 2003. Bristol, UK.

Rose, M. (1995). *Possible lives: The promise of public education in America.* Boston: Houghton Mifflin.

Rose, L. C. & Galup, A. M. (2007, September). The 39th annual Phi Delta Kappa/Gappup Poll of the public's attitudes toward the public schools. *Phi Delta Kappa* 89(1): 33–45.

Rossi, R. (2004, November 30). Civic leaders donating $50 million want accountability from schools. *Chicago Sun Times Online Edition.* Available at: http://wwwsuntimes.com/output/news/cst-nws-renai30.htmlt (accessed December 11, 2007).

Roszak, T. (1968/1995). *The making of a counter culture: Reflections on the technocratic society and its youthful oppositions.* Berkeley: University of California Press.

Ruddick, J. (1991). *Innovation and change.* Milton Keynes, UK: Open University Press.

Rugg, H. (1923). Do the social studies prepare pupils adequately for life activities? In *The twenty-second yearbook of the National Society for the Study of Education, Part II* (pp. 1–27). Bloomington, IL: Public School Publishing Company.

Saltman, K. (2005). *The Edison schools: Corporate schooling and the assault on public education.* New York: Routledge Falmer.

Sassen, S. (1994). *Cities in a world economy.* Thousand Oaks, CA: Pine Forge Press.

Sassen, S. (2004). A global city. In C. Madigan (Ed.), *Global Chicago* (pp. 15–34). Urbana: University of Illinois Press.

Sayer, A. (1995). *Radical political economy: A critique.* Oxford, UK: Blackwell.

Schemo, D. J. (2006, July 19). Republicans propose national school voucher program. *New York Times,* A-17.

Schwarz, J. (2005). *Freedom reclaimed: Rediscovering the American vision.* Baltimore: Johns Hopkins University Press.

Shaw, L. (2004, October 21). U.S. Education Secretary quizzed: Town-hall crowd raises concerns—charter school support elicits boos. *Seattle Times,* B-3.

Shipps, D. (2006). *School reform, corporate style: Chicago 1880–2000.* Lawrence, KS: University of Kansas Press.

Small, A. (1896). Demands of sociology upon pedagogy. *Journal of the Proceedings and Addresses of the Thirty-fifth Annual Meeting of the National Education Association,* 174–184.

Smith, A. (1976). *An inquiry into the nature and causes of the wealth of nations.* R. H. Campell & A .S. Skinner (Eds.) Oxford, UK: Clarendon Press (originally published in 1776).

Smith, N. (1996). *The new urban frontier: Gentrification and the revanchist city.* New York: Routledge.

Smith, N. (2002). New globalism, new urbanism: Gentrification as global urban strategy. *Antipode, 34*(3): 427–450.

Snedden, D. (1915). Vocational education. *New Republic,* 3: 40–42.

Snedden, D. (1924, November 1). Education for a world of team-players and team workers. *School and Society,* 20: 554–556.

Snitzer, H. (1964). *Living at Summerhill: In photographs.* New York: Collier.

Stiglitz, J. (2002). *Globalization and its discontents.* New York: W.W. Norton.

Sunstein, C. (2004). *The second Bill of Rights: FDR's unfinished revolution and why we need it more than ever.* New York: Basic Books.

Tabb, W. (2002). *Unequal partners: A primer on globalization.* New York: New Press.

Taylor, F. W. (1895). A piece-rate system, being a step toward partial solution of the labor problem. *Transactions of the American Society of Mechanical Engineers,* 16: 856–903.

Taylor, F. W. (1911). *Scientific management comprising shop management, the principles of scientific management, testimony before the Special House Committee.* New York: Harper.

Thrupp, M. & Willmott, R. (2003). *Education management in managerialist times: Beyond the textual apologists.* Berkshire, UK: Open University Press.

Tomlinson, S. (2001). Some success, could do better: Education and race 1976–2000. In R. Phillips & J. Furlong (Eds.), *Education, reform and the state: Twenty-five years of politics, policy and practice* (pp. 192–206). New York: Routledge Falmer.

Tyack, D. (1974). *The one best system: A history of American urban education.* Cambridge, MA: Harvard University Press.

U.S. Department of Education, Office of Elementary and Secondary Education. (2002). *No Child Left Behind: A desk reference.* Washington, DC: U.S. Department of Education.

U.S. Department of Education, Office of the Secretary (2003a). *No Child Left Behind: A parents guide.* Washington, DC.

U.S. Department of Education (2003b, August 26). Press release. ABC radio networks launch education campaign to help close achievement gap. Washington, DC. Available at: http://www.ed.gov/news/pressreleases/2003/08/08262003.html (accessed August 29, 2003).

U.S. Department of Education (2006a). *Overview: NCLB is working.* Washington, DC. Available at http://www.ed.gov/nclb/overview/importance/nclbworking.html (accessed December 11, 2007).

U.S. Department of Education (2006b, April 27). Press release. Remarks by Secretary Spellings at No Child Left Behind summit. Washington, DC. Available at: http://www.ed.gov/news/pressreleases/2006/04/04272006.html (accessed December 11, 2007).

U.S. Department of Education, Office of the Press Secretary (2006c, October 5). President Bush discusses No Child Left Behind. Washington, DC. Available at: http://www.whitehouse.gov/news/releases/2006/10/20061005-6.html (accessed December 2, 2007).

Valenzuela, A. (Ed.) (2005). *Leaving children behind: How "Texas-style" accountability fails Latino youth.* Albany, NY: State University of New York Press.

Venkatesh, S. A., Celimli, I., Miller, D., Murphy, A., & Turner, B. (2004, February). *Chicago public housing transformation: A research report.* New York: Center for Urban Research and Policy, Columbia University.

Vidal, J. & Adam, D. (2007, June 19). China overtakes U.S. as world's biggest $CO2$ emitter. *Guardian Unlimited.* Available at: http://www.guardian.co.uk/environment/2007/jun/19/china.usnews (accessed December 2, 2007).

Vilas, C. (1996). Neoliberal social policy: managing poverty (somehow). *NACLA Report on the Americas, 29*(2): 16–21.

Voltaire, F. (2000). *Treatise on tolerance* (B. Masters, Trans., S. Harvey, Ed.). Cambridge, UK: Cambridge University Press (originally published in 1763).

Wacquant, L. (2001). The penalization of poverty and the rise of neoliberalism. *European Journal of Criminal Policy and Research, 9*(4): 401–412.

Ward, L. F. (1883). *The psychic factors of civilization.* Boston: Ginn.

Wells, A. S., Scott, J. T., Lopez, A., & Holme, J. J. (2005). Charter school reform and the shifting meaning of educational equity: Greater voice and greater inequality? In J. Petrovich & A. S. Wells (Eds.), *Bringing equity back: Research for a new era in American educational policy* (pp. 219–243). New York: Teachers College Press.

Weltman, B. (2000, Spring). Revisiting Paul Goodman: Anarcho-snyndicalism as the American way of life. *Educational Theory, 50*(2): 179–200.

Whitty, G., Power, S., & Halpin, D. (1998). *Devolution and choice in education: The school, the state and the market.* Buckingham, UK: Open University Press.

Winerip, M. (2003, August 13). The "zero dropout" miracle: Alas! Alack! A Texas tall tale, *New York Times,* B-7.

Winter, G. (2004, February 26). Minority graduation rates in New York called lowest, *New York Times,* A-3.

Wirth, A. G. (1972). *Education in the technological society: The vocational-liberal studies controversy in the early twentieth century.* Scranton, PA: Intext Educational Publishers.

Wirth, A. G. (1977). Philosophical issues in the vocational-liberal studies controversy (1900–1917): John Dewey vs. the social efficiency philosophers. In A. A. Bellack & H. Kliebard (Eds.) *Curriculum and evaluation* (pp. 161–172). Berkeley, CA: McCutchan.

Wood, G., Darling-Hammond, L., Neill, M. & Roschewski, P. (2007). Refocusing accountability: Using local performance assessments to enhance teaching and learning for higher order skills. Available at: http://www.fairtest.org/nattest/RefocusingAccountability.html (accessed December 2, 2007).

Wrigley, J. (1982). *Class, politics, and public schools: Chicago 1900–1950.* New Brunswick, NJ: Rutgers University Press.

Yerkes, R. (1919, February 15). The mental rating of school children. *National School Service,* 6–7.

Young, I. M. (2000). *Inclusion and democracy.* New York: Oxford University Press.

Index

About the Author

David Hursh is associate professor of teaching and curriculum in the Warner Graduate School of Education at the University of Rochester.